EDINBURGH
UNLOCKED

by
Colin Chisholm

illustrations by
Katherine Hardy

edited by
Emily Kerr & Joshua Perry

WEST...

EAST CENTRAL

NORTH

SOUTH & EAST

WEST

AROUND

TOP FIVES

This book belongs to:

COUNTRY
0 MILES

CITY
0 MILES

FOLLOW ME

WEST CENTRAL

EAST CENTRAL

NORTH

SOUTH & EAST

WEST

AROUND

TOP FIVES

CONTENTS

TIME MACHINE

WEST CENTRAL

EAST CENTRAL

NORTH

SOUTH & EAST

WEST

AROUND

TOP FIVES

MAP OF EDINBURGH

Cramond Island

Newhaven

Leith Docks

Cramond

A902

A900

Barnton

A1140

Portobello

Corstorphine

A8

A199

Newington

Newcraighall

A1

M8

A7

Riccarton

A70

A702

A68

Fairmilehead

Dalkeith

A720

A7

Newtongrange

WEST CENTRAL

EAST CENTRAL

NORTH

SOUTH & EAST

WEST

AROUND

TOP FIVES

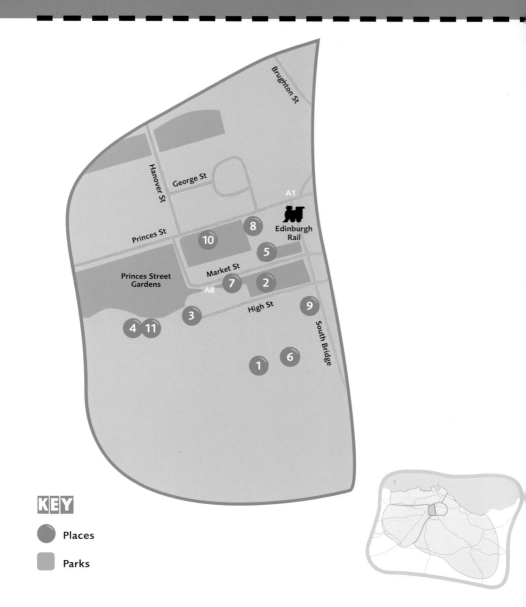

KEY

⬤ Places

⬛ Parks

WEST CENTRAL

EAST CENTRAL

NORTH

SOUTH & EAST

WEST

AROUND

TOP FIVES

FOLLOW ME

H0RR1BL3

MEET EDINBURGH'S MOST FAMOUS DOG

...at the statue of Greyfriars Bobby

Bobby the dog hasn't barked for over 150 years, but his statue remains a big attraction. In fact, he's so famous that there have been two movies made about him. Not many cities can claim to be the birthplace of a film star dog!

Originally Bobby belonged to a man named John Gray. When John died of tuberculosis, Bobby didn't want to leave his master's side, so he spent the rest of his life sitting on John's grave in Greyfriars Kirkyard. He did this for *fourteen whole years*, only leaving to get food.

Sticker Scores

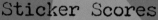

5	4	3
TOP DOG	HANDSOME HOUND	PLAYFUL POOCH

2	1
MISERABLE MUTT	BOTTOM DOG

Bobby's story became famous and after his death a lady paid for the statue to be erected. Now people come to pat his head and pay their respects to his dogged devotion!

Best Of The Rest

🔑 Take a walk into Greyfriars Kirkyard and pay your respects at Greyfriars Bobby's gravestone, near the main gates. Bobby is thought to have been buried around here, though the exact spot is not known.

🔑 While you're in the graveyard, make sure you also search for John Gray's grave. It's on the graveyard's eastern path.

Photo Op
Get a snap of you standing beside Bobby stroking his head. You'd be barking mad not to!

"I wonder when he's coming back?"

Fascinating Facts

⭐ Bobby's devotion was not immediately appreciated. Soon after John Gray's death the man in charge of the graveyard tried to chase him away. However, he eventually befriended Bobby and even brought the little dog a blanket to keep him warm at night!

⭐ Apparently, the statue used to face the other way, but a canny pub owner turned it round so that his pub would always appear in the thousands of photos that are taken with Bobby each year.

⭐ Bobby's original collar and bowl can be found in the Edinburgh Museum (see p36).

PLAN YOUR VISIT ①

Greyfriars Bobby
Corner of George IV Bridge and Candlemaker Row
www.greyfriarsbobby.co.uk
FREE

I want to go here ☐

WEST CENTRAL
EAST CENTRAL
NORTH
SOUTH & EAST
WEST
AROUND
TOP FIVES

EXPLORE AN UNDERGROUND STREET

...in Mary King's Close

Roads are normally at ground level. That's kind of the point. But buried under Edinburgh's Royal Mile is a mysterious network of *underground* streets that were forgotten for hundreds of years . . .

Mary King's Close is one of four small ancient streets that were discovered under the modern-day city of Edinburgh, and opened to the public in 2003. The people who lived there in the 1600s got the plague, a really nasty disease that killed almost everyone who caught it. You can visit the home of a grave digger's family to discover what life was like living with the plague. Some people say that a few plague victims are still down there haunting the tiny streets . . .

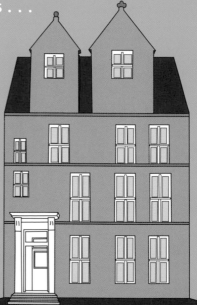

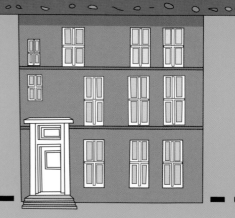

Sticker Scores

5 TERRIFYING TERRACE

4 SCARY STREET

3 PHANTOM PLACE

2 GHOSTLY GARDENS

1 RING ROAD

WEST CENTRAL

EAST CENTRAL

NORTH

SOUTH & EAST

WEST

AROUND

TOP FIVES

Best Of The Rest

🔑 Take a ghostly tour of the close. On Saturday evenings between November and March you can go on supernatural tours. But be warned – it will send a shiver down your spine!

🔑 Other special tours include Christmas at the Close during December, and an Old Town Walking Tour.

Top Tip
You need to book trips to the close in advance as places on the guided tours are limited.

← This way for a hidden street

Fascinating Facts

⭐ **The plague was a very nasty disease which was quite common in old Edinburgh. It caused big, pustular spots, and would often kill people who were unlucky enough to catch it.**

⭐ People who caught the plague would stay inside their house and put a small white flag in the window. Kind passers-by would then see the flag and leave food and water at the door.

⭐ **During World War Two, Mary King's Close was used as an air raid shelter. So, though many people once died in the plague-infested close, during the war it actually helped save lives!**

⭐ On your tour you'll see Annie's room, which is said to contain the ghost of a sad, lonely young girl. Visitors sometimes leave toys in her room to cheer her up.

PLAN YOUR VISIT ②

The Real Mary King's Close
2 Warriston's Close, EH1 1PG
www.realmarykingsclose.com

📞 0845 070 6244

🕐 Tours depart daily (summer) 09.00-21.00
Daily (out of season) 10.00-17.00
(pre-booking essential)

££ 🎁 ☂

I want to go here ☐

GO INSIDE A GIANT CAMERA

...at Camera Obscura and World of Illusions

How would you like to pick up passers-by in the palm of your hand? Or use a piece of paper to lift a car? Well, both are (sort of) possible at the **Camera Obscura and World of Illusions.**

Sticker Scores

5	4	3
BRIGHT LIGHTS	CLEAR SKY	FLICKERING BULB

2	1
TWILIGHT	LIGHTS OUT

A Camera Obscura is a clever way to see moving images without using any electronic trickery. You go inside the giant camera and live pictures of Edinburgh are projected on the table in front of you from a small hole in the side of the building. Put your hand in front of the hole and the image will be projected onto your skin. Anyone and anything is within your grasp!

WEST CENTRAL

EAST CENTRAL

NORTH

SOUTH & EAST

WEST

AROUND

TOP FIVES

Best Of The Rest

🔑 Check out the giant holograms, bendy mirrors and weird lenses in the World of Illusions exhibition, which is next to the Camera Obscura. What you see is definitely not what you get!

🔑 Turn into a chimp! Take your photo on the morph machine, and then you can morph into a chimp, a baby, or even one of your friends . . .

← Inside a camera obscura

Photo Op
Swap heads with a friend in the World of Illusions mirror gallery and take a photo of you wearing each other's face!

Top Tip
Don't forget to take your camera with you for the breathtaking views from the rooftop.

Fascinating Facts

★ The Camera Obscura is a pinhole camera. Light comes in through a small hole and makes an image appear. Cavemen were using the same principle thousands of years ago (although probably not to pick up cars).

★ Pinhole camera images appear upside down. This is because light can only travel in a straight line. So, light coming from low down outside the camera enters the pinhole and keeps travelling in a straight line up high to the top of the image. You get a perfect picture, but it's the wrong way up!

PLAN YOUR VISIT ③

Camera Obscura and World Of Illusions

Castlehill, The Royal Mile, EH1 2ND
www.camera-obscura.co.uk

📞 0131 226 3709

🕐 Daily (summer) 09.30-19.30
Daily (out-of-season) 10.00-17.00

££ 🎁 ☂

I want to go here ☐

TELL THE TIME WITH A GUN

...at Edinburgh Castle

Most people tell the time with watches, clocks, or mobile phones. But Edinburgh Castle ignores these traditional techniques. Instead they use a massive cannon that can be heard for miles around!

The cannon is positioned on the north side of the castle at the Mills Mount Battery. It is fired as part of a tradition called the one o'clock gun. This used to help sailors in the Port of Leith tell the time.

In the old days, ships would navigate at night using the stars. However, as the world turns and the time changes, the stars also change their positions in the sky. This meant sailors needed to know the exact time to be able to work out their route accurately. The one o'clock gun allowed them to keep their clocks correct.

Sticker Scores

5 TOP GUN

4 COOL CANNON

3 CRACKING CLOCK

2 STOP WATCH

1 STOPPED WATCH

WEST CENTRAL

EAST CENTRAL

NORTH

SOUTH & EAST

WEST

AROUND

TOP FIVES

Best Of The Rest

🔑 The castle is home to the Crown Jewels of Scotland and the Stone of Scone, which Scottish kings used to be crowned on.

🔑 You can also visit the castle's dingy dungeons and the Great Hall, where fancy banquets took place.

Top Tip

Make your way to the Mills Mount Battery just before one o'clock and look down over the shoppers on Princes Street as the gun fires and they jump with surprise!

← Edinburgh Castle

Fascinating Facts

⭐ A local legend says that during the late nineteenth century a group of soldiers at Edinburgh Castle decided to fire the one o'clock gun at one in the morning. Something went wrong with the mechanism, and the gun flew backwards to reveal a secret passage! The first man who went down was never seen again. And nor, for that matter, was the secret passage . . .

⭐ In 1720, 21 pirates were thrown into the castle dungeons and then hanged.

⭐ Edinburgh has a gun and a time ball (see p39) which both mark one o'clock. The gun is there in case the sailors couldn't see the time ball through the mist.

PLAN YOUR VISIT ④

Edinburgh Castle
Castle Hill, EH1 2NG
www.edinburghcastle.gov.uk

📞 0131 225 9846

🕐 Daily (summer) 09.30-18.00
Daily (winter) 09.20-17.00
Gun fires at 13.00

I want to go here ☐

HANG AROUND

...at the Edinburgh Dungeon

Do you fancy 'hanging around' with murderers and criminals? Well you can at the Edinburgh Dungeon. Take the Extremis drop ride and you'll be sent down into the abyss by a hooded hangman!

The Edinburgh Dungeon explains the bloodiest bits of Edinburgh's history. You'll hear about Burke and Hare (and Burke's horrible hanging), and find out about the story of William Wallace, a patriotic Scot who fought the English before being hung, drawn and quartered. *Ouch*!

Sticker Scores

⭐ 5	⭐ 4	⭐ 3
DRAMATIC DUNGEON	COLD CAVERN	GROTTY GROTTO

⭐ 2	⭐ 1
ABYSMAL ABYSS	PONGING PRISON

The Extremis ride is the bit where you too get to be hanged. You defend yourself before a bloodthirsty judge who condemns you to death (whether you're guilty or not!). Hold on as you hurtle down into the darkness below . . .

WEST CENTRAL

EAST CENTRAL

NORTH

SOUTH & EAST

WEST

AROUND

TOP FIVES

Best Of The Rest

As part of your journey around the dungeon, you'll take a boat ride into the Galloway cave. This all sounds rather jolly, until you find out that the cave is the hiding place of Sawny Bean, the head of a family of cannibals. Mind your head!

Photo Op
Snap yourself cutting off your parents' heads! There's a chance for you to put an adult in the stocks, then take a picture of you cutting their heads off with an axe!

← You'll be hooked . . . .

Fascinating Facts

★ William Brodie was a respected Edinburgh tradesman who designed a gibbet (wooden frame for hanging people) in 1777. However, William also had a secret life as a burglar. When he was caught, he was convicted and sentenced to death on the gibbet of his own devising!

★ Burke and Hare killed seventeen people in Edinburgh in the early 1800s. They then sold the dead bodies to the devious Doctor Knox who used them for medical research!

What did the executioner do with his pen and paper?
Wrote a *chopping* list!

PLAN YOUR VISIT 5

The Edinburgh Dungeon
31 Market Street, EH1 1QB
www.thedungeons.com

📞 0131 240 1001

🕐 Daily (summer) 10.00-19.00
Opening hours vary out of season

£££

I want to go here ☐

DRIVE A FORMULA ONE RACING CAR

...at the National Museum of Scotland

Here's your chance to see if you could be the next Jenson Button or Lewis Hamilton. At the National Museum of Scotland you can drive a lap in a Formula One simulator!

The National Museum of Scotland tells the story of Scotland's people, history and culture. Its exhibits include everything from ancient fossils to a dead sheep called Dolly!

Formula One features here because one of the greatest racing drivers of all time, Jackie Stewart, comes from Scotland. He also used to own an F1 team, and a real 1998 Stewart F1 car is positioned next to the simulator. As you drive you'll pass famous Scottish landmarks like Loch Ness and Ben Nevis. Just make sure they don't distract you from the road!

Sticker Scores

5 RAPID RACER

4 TERRIFIC TOURER

3 DECENT DASHER

2 DODGY DRIVER

1 BROKEN DOWN

WEST CENTRAL

EAST CENTRAL

NORTH

SOUTH & EAST

WEST

AROUND

TOP FIVES

Best Of The Rest

🔑 As well as racing an F1 car, you can also design your own racing car in the Move It part of the Connect Gallery.

🔑 Alternatively, why not put on a spacesuit and go for a moonwalk in the Blast Off! section?

🔑 Or, if you're feeling practical, design your own robot in the Robots section. You can choose to make one that cleans the house or defuses bombs. Just don't get them mixed up – or you might explode the dishwasher!

← Time for a pit stop

Fascinating Facts

⭐ The fastest ever road car is the SSC Ultimate Aero. It is even swifter than a Formula One car and has a top speed of 257 miles per hour! That's three and a half times faster than you're allowed to drive on the motorway . . .

⭐ Dolly the sheep is famous because she was the first ever mammal to be 'cloned'. This means that she wasn't born in the normal way, but was created by Scottish scientists using a skin cell from another sheep.

Top Tip
You'll need to be over 137cm tall to use the simulator – otherwise you can't reach the pedals.

PLAN YOUR VISIT 6

National Museum of Scotland
Chamber Street, EH1 1JF
www.nms.ac.uk
📞 0131 225 7534
🕐 Daily 10.00-17.00
FREE ✕ 🎁 ☂ ❗

I want to go here ☐

CRACK OPEN A SAFE

...at the Museum on the Mound

Don't worry, we're not suggesting you do anything illegal. At the Museum on the Mound, you can have a go at cracking open a safe without getting arrested!

The museum is inside the headquarters of the Bank of Scotland. Visiting a bank may not sound like a brilliant way to spend a day, but this one is different. It's full of hands-on activities such as coin rubbing and building a model bank.

We particularly like the safe-cracking challenge.

Sticker Scores

5	4	3
TOP DOLLAR	PERFECT POUND	SUPER CENT

2	1
COPPER COIN	SPEND A PENNY

You solve the clues to find the correct combination and then open the safe by moving the dial. Get it right and you even get to keep the goodies inside! *Banks* very much . . .

WEST CENTRAL

EAST CENTRAL

NORTH

SOUTH & EAST

WEST

AROUND

TOP FIVES

Best Of The Rest

🔑 See a million pounds in a case near the safe! Sadly you don't get to keep it.

🔑 Check out Scotland's oldest surviving banknote – it's nearly 300 years old!

← Get your hands on the goodies

"Why did you swallow that 50p I gave you?"
"You said it was my lunch money!"

Fascinating Facts

★ Metal was first used as money at least 4,000 years ago when people began to make payments with silver and gold. Before that, people used valuable items like shells, furs, tea, salt and even cows as a form of currency. However, this was not ideal – cows are more likely than coins to run away, and are also harder to fit in your pocket.

★ Scotland had its own currency until 1707, when the parliaments of England and Scotland joined together. Nowadays both countries use the pound sterling, though Scotland still prints its own banknotes.

★ The pound gets its name from the weight once used to measure money. Originally, 240 silver pennies weighed a pound.

PLAN YOUR VISIT ⑦

Museum on the Mound
The Mound, EH1 1YZ
www.museumonthemound.com

📞 0131 243 5464

🕐 Tue-Fri 10.00-17.00
Sat-Sun, 13.00-17.00

FREE

I want to go here ☐

TAKE A HORRIBLE BUS TOUR

...on an open-top bus

Just to be clear, we're not suggesting that bus tours are horrible! In fact, they're a great way to see Edinburgh. And they're even better when the commentary is provided by *Horrible Histories*!

There are four different tours on open-top buses around the city. You can get on and off whenever you like, and you can always shelter downstairs if the famous Edinburgh mist (or haar) arrives.

Our favourite is City Sightseeing Tours because of their *Horrible Histories* audio guide. You'll hear author Terry Deary tell you about the cruel characters and terrible tales that make up Edinburgh's past. And, if it's all getting a bit too gruesome, you can always hop off and come back later!

Sticker Scores

5 BRILLIANT BUS

4 TERRIFIC TRAIN

3 COMFORTABLE COACH

2 TERRIBLE TRAM

1 *BUS*-TED!

H0RR1BL3

WEST CENTRAL

EAST CENTRAL

NORTH

SOUTH & EAST

WEST

AROUND

TOP FIVES

Best Of The Rest

🔑 Take the Edinburgh Tour if you'd like to listen to a real guide.

🔑 Choose Mactours if you'd like to travel in a vintage bus.

🔑 Opt for Majestic Tours if you want to go to HMY *Britannia* (see p62) – they are the only ones that go that far.

Top Tip

Edinburgh's weather can be a bit dodgy even in the summer so have a jacket handy for the top deck.

The history's horrible but the bus isn't →

Why did the bus driver win the race?

He had a good coach!

Fascinating Facts

★ Until the 1920s virtually all double-decker buses were made without a roof on the top deck. However, before too long the bus companies realised that people like it better when they're not getting wetter!

★ Buses get their name from the Latin word 'omnibus', meaning 'for all'. Before buses, only posh people could afford to travel across town by anything other than foot. It was not until horse and steam powered bus services started to appear in the 1800s that the ordinary person got to join in with the transport revolution.

PLAN YOUR VISIT ⑧

Edinburgh Bus Tours
Waverley Bridge (for all four companies), EH1 1BQ
www.edinburghtour.com

📞 0131 220 0770

££

I want to go here ☐

VENTURE INTO A HAUNTED VAULT

...with Mercat Tours

The vaults under South Bridge have been called one of the most haunted places in Britain. All kinds of unexplained things keep happening there. Take this tour to find out more . . .

Mercat offer a range of guided tours across Edinburgh. If you go on one of their ghost walks you'll learn all about the gorier parts of Edinburgh's history. You'll also find out about the development of the city's eerie underground vaults.

Built in the 1700s, the vaults were originally store rooms which merchants used to keep food and drink fresh. Later they were used by beggars and thieves. On the tour, a guide will tell you about how you might sense ghosts here, using smell, sound or touch. Are you brave enough?

Sticker Scores

5 GHASTLY GHOST

4 SPOOKY SPIRIT

3 AWFUL APPARITION

2 FEARFUL PHANTOM

1 SCAREDY CAT

WEST CENTRAL

EAST CENTRAL

NORTH

SOUTH & EAST

WEST

AROUND

TOP FIVES

Best Of The Rest

If ghosts aren't your thing, you can choose to take a Mercat Historic Vaults tour instead. You'll still see the vaults, but with fewer tales of the paranormal!

Alternatively, stay above ground on one of the company's Secrets of the Royal Mile tours.

Why are ghosts no good at telling lies?

Because you can see right through them!

← Edinburgh's eerie underground vaults

Fascinating Facts

★ The Mercat Cross, where the tour starts from, used to be a place for public torture and punishments. Locals would come to watch for some free entertainment. Fortunately, people's idea of a good time has changed since then!

★ Mercat is an old Scots word for market. Many Scottish towns have a 'mercat cross' to mark the place where the market was held. The word has nothing to do with meerkats – a type of small mongoose. Just in case you were wondering.

★ South Bridge has nineteen stone arches, but eighteen of them are now hidden from view by other buildings that have been constructed either side. The arch that is still visible today is above Cowgate.

PLAN YOUR VISIT 9

Mercat Tours Ghost Tours
28 Blair Street, EH1 1QR
www.mercattours.com

℡ 0131 225 5445

🕐 Daily tours 14.15-21.00
Advance tickets available online

££

I want to go here ☐

GLIDE IN THE GARDENS

...at Edinburgh's Winter Wonderland

Every winter, Princes Street Gardens are transformed into a Winter Wonderland, complete with ice rink, fairground and market. It's *snow* joke!

The gardens actually used to be a swamp called the Nor Loch. It was the place where the people of Edinburgh would dump . . . well, everything! We definitely think that the gardens are a big improvement on a rubbish tip.

Sticker Scores

5 ICE RINK

4 I SHRINK

3 I BLINK

2 I THINK

1 I STINK

You'll be able to show off your skating skills on the ice rink, which is one of the biggest outdoor skating venues in the UK. And even better, you can enjoy the dramatic views of Edinburgh Castle as you glide along or fall over, depending on your ability!

WEST CENTRAL

EAST CENTRAL

NORTH

SOUTH & EAST

WEST

AROUND

TOP FIVES

Best Of The Rest

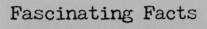

During your visit you can boing in the bungee dome, fly round the ferris wheel or just meander about the market.

Warm up with hot drinks and mince pies, which can be bought from the various food stands.

Top Tip

If you're not a confident skater then head to the practice rink where the marshals will give you some helpful hints.

What do you get if you cross a snowman and a shark?

Frosthite!

← Skating on not-so-thin ice

Fascinating Facts

⭐ Christmas Day wasn't an official holiday in Scotland until the 1960s. Until then Hogmanay (the Scottish word for New Year) was considered a better excuse for a day off.

⭐ Each year, Edinburgh hosts a massive street party for Hogmanay. The highest ever attendance was 300,000 – that's almost as many people as actually live in Edinburgh.

⭐ Ice skating features in the Winter Olympics in many different forms. Speed skating (skating very fast), figure skating (a mixture of skating and dancing) and ice hockey (playing hockey and bashing into people while on skates) are all popular events.

PLAN YOUR VISIT 10

Winter Wonderland

East Princes Street Gardens

www.gildedballoon.co.uk/wwonderland

📞 0131 662 6552

🕐 Sun-Wed (winter) 10.00-20.00
Thu-Sat (winter) 10.00-22.00

I want to go here ☐

TRY A TATTOO

...at the Edinburgh Military Tattoo

Tattoos don't have to involve having patterns drawn on your body! In Edinburgh the word more commonly refers to marching soldiers . . .

The Edinburgh Military Tattoo is one of the most famous things about the city. The performance involves lots of soldiers marching together while playing bagpipes and drums. It all takes place next to Edinburgh Castle, with dramatic lights and lasers adding to the spectacle.

The Tattoo only runs during August and because it's so popular tickets are hard to get and have to be bought a long time in advance. So book early if you want to view a tattoo!

Sticker Scores

5 BRILLIANT BRIGADES

4 UPLIFTING UNITS

3 COLOURFUL COMPANIES

2 BLAND BANDS

1 TUNELESS TROOPS

WEST CENTRAL

EAST CENTRAL

NORTH

SOUTH & EAST

WEST

AROUND

TOP FIVES

Fascinating Facts

⭐ The idea of a military tattoo dates back to the 1600s when drummers from the British army would play in pubs while fighting in the Netherlands. They were allowed to continue until the bartender called 'Doe den tap toe' meaning 'Turn off the taps'. The Brits, who have never had a reputation for being brilliant at languages, thought this sounded a bit like 'tattoo', and the name stuck.

⭐ Ink tattoos may have been around for 10,000 years. Neolithic men were found with primitive carbon tattoos on their bodies.

⭐ In 2003 a Russian female duo called Tatu had a number one hit in the UK with a song called All The Things She Said. The band members had no visible tattoos and did not play any drums or bagpipes.

Pipers at the tattoo

Top Tip
Tattoo tickets go on sale at the start of December so try to buy them as soon as they're available.

Photo Op
Find a cake tin and a couple of twigs and have your photo taken pretending to be a military drummer!

PLAN YOUR VISIT 11

Edinburgh Military Tattoo
Castle Esplanade, EH1 9GB
www.edintattoo.co.uk

📞 0131 225 1188

🕐 Mon-Fri 21.00, Sat 19.30 & 22.30 (August only)

£££

I want to go here ☐

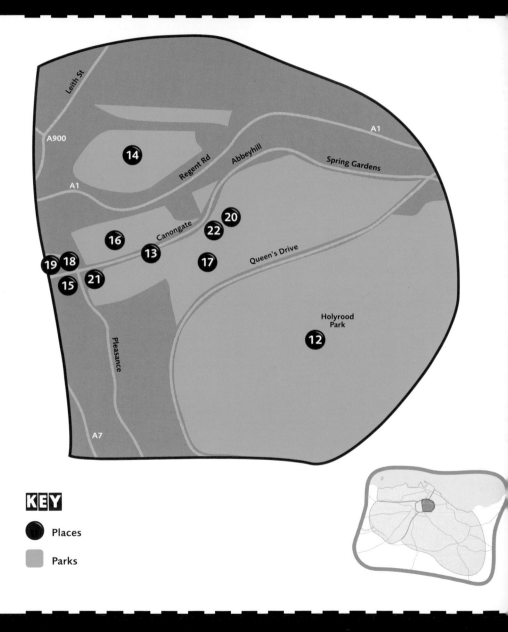

KEY

- **Places**
- **Parks**

WEST CENTRAL

EAST CENTRAL

NORTH

SOUTH & EAST

WEST

AROUND

TOP FIVES

CLIMB A VOLCANO

...at Arthur's Seat

Climbing a volcano might sound dangerous, but Arthur's Seat has been extinct for 350 million years so you're unlikely to be covered in lava. The walk is well worth the effort – the summit has the best view in Edinburgh!

Arthur's Seat is a mini-volcano in Holyrood Park, in the centre of Edinburgh. Some people say it was named after King Arthur, the legendary British king, but no one is sure. What is certain is that it was a good defensive position – you can still see the remains of prehistoric forts surrounding the hill. The walk to the top and back can take an hour, so make sure you wear appropriate clothes. (And no, we don't mean a suit of armour!)

Sticker Scores

5 VOLCANIC LAVA

4 BOILING WATER

3 STEAMY SHOWER

2 LUKEWARM LAKE

1 ICE BATH

WEST CENTRAL

EAST CENTRAL

NORTH

SOUTH & EAST

WEST

AROUND

TOP FIVES

Top Tip

Climb to the top from the north or west side if you're feeling full of beans. Alternatively, for a gentler walk, drive to Dunsapie Loch and start on the east side.

Why do volcanoes get married?
Because they *lava* each other!

← Edinburgh's (hopefully) extinct volcano

Photo Op

If it's not too windy, get a snap of you standing on the stone at the summit. You may need a grown-up to hold on to – it's a long way down if you fall!

Fascinating Facts

⭐ Like Rome, Edinburgh is supposed to be built on seven hills. Arthur's Seat is one of them. See if you can spot the other six from the top. (Mole hills don't count.)

⭐ Arthur's Seat is 251 metres tall. That's as tall as an 80 storey building, or 150 knights standing on each others' shoulders (but less likely to be wearing armour).

⭐ In the 1900s, people who owed money would hide in Holyrood Park. Because the park was private property owned by the Royal family, the police could not arrest them!

PLAN YOUR VISIT 12

Arthur's Seat

Holyrood Park, EH16 5BT

FREE

I want to go here ☐

BUILD YOUR OWN ROYAL MILE

...at the Museum of Edinburgh

The Royal Mile is a collection of streets in Edinburgh which together are (unsurprisingly) about a mile long. It's the city's most famous street, and so it's a perfect place to pick up a souvenir . . .

The Museum of Edinburgh is on the Royal Mile, and its exhibits tell the fascinating, funny and sometimes bloody story of Edinburgh's history. It also has a great activity area, where you can build your own Royal Mile!

Use the card and colouring pencils provided to make miniature models.

Or, if that sounds a bit fiddly, you can create a collage or try a silver rubbing. There are loads of buildings to choose from – will your creations look as impressive as the real ones?

Sticker Scores

5 AMAZING ARTEFACTS

4 ROCKING REMAINS

3 INTERESTING ITEMS

2 DECENT DISPLAYS

1 CRUMMY COLLECTION

Best Of The Rest

🔑 Check out Greyfriars Bobby's bowl and collar, which are kept here in the museum. He was Edinburgh's most famous dog (see p10).

🔑 Dress up in costumes from old Edinburgh. You could be a lawyer, a doctor or even a washerwoman. Just make sure that nobody tries to give you their dirty clothes!

🔑 If you fancy a bit of peace and quiet, head to the reading corner and browse some interesting books.

Top Tip
Go to the activity area before visiting the rest of the museum and pick up a free activity trail to guide you around.

← A sundial outside the Museum of Edinburgh

Fascinating Facts

★ The site of the Museum of Edinburgh has had many uses. Before the current building was constructed, it was home to a well, a brewery and even a manure heap! Thankfully it no longer pongs of poo . . .

★ Confusingly, the Scots used to have their own mile measurement, called a Scots mile. It was around 1,800 metres long (compared to 1,609 metres for a standard mile), though it varied in length depending on who was doing the measuring! The Royal Mile is about one Scots mile long.

Photo Op
Get dressed up in your favourite costume, then pose for the camera.

PLAN YOUR VISIT 13

Museum of Edinburgh
Huntly House,142 Canongate, EH8 8DD
www.edinburgh.gov.uk/museums

📞 0131 529 4143

🕐 Mon-Sat 10.00-17.00
Sun (Aug only) 12.00-17.00

I want to go here ☐

WEST CENTRAL
EAST CENTRAL
NORTH
SOUTH & EAST
WEST
AROUND
TOP FIVES

FLY A KITE IN THE CITY CENTRE

...on Calton Hill

Edinburgh is sometimes called The Windy City – which is good news if you're a fan of flying kites! One of the best places to go is Calton Hill, right in the middle of town.

Nowadays Calton Hill is full of tourists and kites, but 500 years ago it was mostly used by knights on horseback to hold jousting tournaments. It also had a monastery (a place where monks lived), a hospital and a prison on it. The most famous construction still standing on Calton Hill is the National Monument, which looks ruined but actually was just never finished. Make sure your kite doesn't get tangled in its columns!

Sticker Scores

5 TERRIBLE TORNADO

4 ROARING GALE

3 STIFF BREEZE

2 GENTLE GUST

1 TRAPPED WIND

WEST CENTRAL

EAST CENTRAL

NORTH

SOUTH & EAST

WEST

AROUND

TOP FIVES

Best Of The Rest

Watch a time ball drop on the Nelson Monument, which is also on Calton Hill. The giant time ball helped people to tell the time in the days before accurate watches.

← The unfinished National Monument

Top Tip

If you don't have a kite, head to Another Planet, Edinburgh's specialist kite shop on Ashley Terrace (www.another-planet.com). They stock everything from beginner kites to super stunt models.

Photo Op

Try to catch the time ball as it drops at 13.00. You'll need good reflexes – snap a second too late and you'll miss it!

Fascinating Facts

★ The reason the National Monument is unfinished is that the funding ran out after they started to build it – and no money meant no monument!

★ Since 1852 the time ball on the Nelson Monument has dropped down at 13.00 exactly. It is situated on top of a hill so that even sailors out at sea could see it drop and know what time it was at least once a day.

★ Each summer, the hill is host to the Beltane Fire Festival. People light torches and a huge bonfire and march around the hill. It's great fun – just don't try to recreate the festival in your back garden . . .

PLAN YOUR VISIT **14**

Calton Hill
Regent Road, EH1 3DG

FREE

I want to go here ☐

SEARCH FOR A ROYAL TOY

...in the Museum of Childhood

In 1955 a councillor had a brainwave. Lots of museums tell the story of grown-up history, he thought; why not establish a museum about the lives of children? And so, the world's first museum of childhood was opened in Edinburgh . . .

Councillor Murray was spurred into action because there was no space anywhere else in Scotland to show Queen Victoria's dolls. Now the museum is full of all kinds of children's toys and games, from teddies to trains to tricycles.

Sticker Scores

5 DELIGHTFUL DOLL

4 ROCKING HORSE

3 TERRIFIC TRICYCLE

2 TROUBLESOME TEDDY

1 BORED GAME

If you fancy a challenge, why not become a toy hunter? Ask at reception and the museum will give you clues to find toys from all over the world, including the royal dolls.

Best Of The Rest

🔑 Play Snakes and Ladders in the museum's board game section.

🔑 Nose around a 1930s classroom where you'll hear children chanting their times tables and running around in the playground.

🔑 While you're visiting the classroom you can also dress up as a child from the 1930s. Pick your favourite outfit and imagine you were born 80 years ago!

> Why don't teddy bears ever eat anything? Because they're always *stuffed.*

Fascinating Facts

⭐ **During Victorian times in Edinburgh many families couldn't afford to buy toys and dolls. Instead they made their own using sticks, clothes pegs and old clothes. Lucky children from wealthy families had rocking horses, or dolls made of fancy china and wax.**

⭐ Queen Victoria was a lonely child. Her guardians developed a strict set of rules to prevent her from meeting other children. They were so protective that she had to share a bedroom with her mother every night until she became Queen at eighteen!

⭐ **The young Victoria kept herself entertained by playing with her doll's house, keeping pets and riding horses. Her closest companion was a dog called Dash.**

← Entrance to the Museum of Childhood

PLAN YOUR VISIT 15

The Museum of Childhood
42 High Street, Royal Mile, EH1 1TG
www.edinburgh.gov.uk/museums

📞 0131 529 4142

🕐 Mon-Sat 10.00-17.00, Sun 12.00-17.00

FREE

I want to go here ☐

WEST CENTRAL

EAST CENTRAL

NORTH

SOUTH & EAST

WEST

AROUND

TOP FIVES

MEET THE TERRIBLE TOWN GUARD

...at the People's Story Museum

The Town Guard were both hated and feared by the people of Edinburgh. Before there was a police force these 'men in red' were in charge of crime and punishment.

Inside the People's Story you'll see one of the guardsmen for yourself. You can find out about the horrible tortures and executions they used to carry out and peek inside a prison cell.

You might also meet the Town Crier, who announces the fate of inmates. Those who committed the most serious crimes could expect a grisly death. Luckier ones would be sent halfway round the world to Australia. (Hundreds of years ago that was considered a punishment!)

Sticker Scores

5 PERFECT PLOT

4 CUNNING CRIME

3 MISCHIEVOUS MISDEED

2 SILLY SCHEME

1 FEEBLE FELONY

WEST CENTRAL

EAST CENTRAL

NORTH

SOUTH & EAST

WEST

AROUND

TOP FIVES

Best Of The Rest

Check out the stag on the side of the Canongate Tolbooth clock. This was the symbol of the Canongate district. It comes from the legend of King David of Scotland, who was supposedly attacked by a stag but managed to fight it off. What a *stag*-gering achievement!

Walk round a graveyard in nearby Canongate Kirkyard. Many famous Scots are buried here, including Adam Smith who lived in the 1700s. Adam came up with some clever ideas about how economies and businesses work. Sadly, he offered no advice on how to get your parents to increase your pocket money.

← Extra, extra, read all about it!

Fascinating Facts

★ The People's Story is located in the Canongate Tolbooth – the oldest building still standing on the Canongate. This used to be the main council building, where people paid their tolls and taxes. It also used to contain a courtroom and a prison.

★ Most of the town guardsmen were from the Highlands, in the north of Scotland. The fact they were from out of town was one of the reasons they were so unpopular. Thankfully these days the locals are more welcoming to people who aren't from Edinburgh!

How do you join the town guards? Handcuff them together!

PLAN YOUR VISIT 16

The People's Story Museum
Canongate Tolbooth, 163 Canongate, EH8 8BN
www.edinburgh.gov.uk/museums

📞 0131 529 4057

🕐 Mon-Sat 10.00-17.00
Sun (August only) 12.00-17.00

FREE

I want to go here ☐

TRAVEL BACK IN TIME

...at Our Dynamic Earth

We're guessing you're unlikely to have a time machine at home. So why not use the one at Our Dynamic Earth? Travel back 13.75 billion years and see the universe being made!

TIME MACHINE

Sticker Scores

⭐ 5 — STUNNING SUPERNOVA

⭐ 4 — PRETTY PULSAR

⭐ 3 — NORMAL NEBULA

⭐ 2 — DREARY DWARF

⭐ 1 — SORRY STAR

OK, so Our Dynamic Earth doesn't really have a time machine (though if it did it would be really useful at bedtime!). What it does have is a very cool lift which transports you past events from history covering millions of years. Once you've left the time machine you'll end up on the bridge of a spaceship where you can watch the Big Bang happening. See galaxies generated, planets produced and stars started, all from a safe distance . . .

WEST CENTRAL

EAST CENTRAL

NORTH

SOUTH & EAST

WEST

AROUND

TOP FIVES

Best Of The Rest

🔑 There are plenty of interesting exhibits at Our Dynamic Earth. You can feel a fossil in the Casualties and Survivors gallery, inspect an iceberg in Polar Extremes or roam round a rainforest in the Tropical Rainforest gallery.

← Part museum, part time machine

How do you transport herbs into the future? With a thyme machine!

Photo Op
Get a snap of you with your head in the mouth of the sabre-toothed tiger in the Casualties and Survivors gallery!

Fascinating Facts

⭐ **The Big Bang is the name people use to describe the events that led to the creation of the universe. Though nobody knows for sure, the theory is that at some point billions of years ago there must have been no universe. Then, suddenly the universe appeared, and it has been expanding ever since. Confused? Well, so are many scientists still.**

⭐ Time travel may become a reality in the future. The scientist Albert Einstein developed the Theory of Special Relativity, which demonstrates that time travel is possible, at least in theory. However, so far no one has managed to achieve it . . . yet! So Our Dynamic Earth is still the best way to take a trip through time.

PLAN YOUR VISIT 17

Our Dynamic Earth
Holyrood Road, EH8 8AS
www.dynamicearth.co.uk

📞 0131 550 7800

🕐 Daily (summer) 10.00-18.00
Wed-Sun (out of season) 10.00-17.00

I want to go here ☐

FIND A GREAT BEDTIME STORY

...at the Scottish Storytelling Centre

Once upon a time there was a building and public courtyard dedicated to stories from Scotland. Actually, we're rubbish at telling stories, so we won't even try. Instead, we'll tell you about a place that is very good at it indeed.

The Scottish Storytelling Centre is dedicated to live tale-telling, and regularly has a storyteller in the court area. You can listen to tremendous tales, many with music and songs, and join in with other activities.

Our favourite bit is the stupendous story wall. You'll find mini-stories and models hidden behind doors and cupboards. Look out for William Wallace (a fearsome fighter and national hero), or Oor Wullie (a spiky-haired comic book character).

Sticker Scores

5 TERRIFIC TALE

4 AWESOME ACCOUNT

3 STORMING STORY

2 USELESS YARN

1 FEEBLE FABLE

WEST CENTRAL

EAST CENTRAL

NORTH

SOUTH & EAST

WEST

AROUND

TOP FIVES

Best Of The Rest

🔑 Solve a picture puzzle at John Knox House, which is part of the Storytelling Centre complex. In one of the puzzles, you rearrange the pieces to make portraits of famous Scottish folk and see how they met their end.

🔑 Hunt for the site of the old Netherbow Port, just next to the Scottish Storytelling Centre. This is where the old east gate of Edinburgh city used to be. Brass cobbles on the ground show where it once stood.

← Tell me a story

Top Tip
Check the website before you go to check when the when the storytelling sessions are scheduled.

Fascinating Facts

★ One of Scotland's most famous storytellers is a writer called Robert Louis Stevenson. His most popular book, *Treasure Island*, was written to help entertain his thirteen year old stepson on a summer holiday. You can hear some of it in the audio bothy (a Scottish word for a little hut or alcove).

★ John Knox House is one of Edinburgh's oldest buildings, dating from the 1400s. The Storytelling Centre building was opened in 2006 and is one of the newest. See which one you prefer!

Top Tip
If you've got a story you really like write it down and add it to the postbox on the Story Wall.

PLAN YOUR VISIT 18

Scottish Storytelling Centre
43-45 High Street, EH1 1SR
www.scottishstorytellingcentre.co.uk
📞 0131 336 9579
🕐 Mon-Sat 10.00-18.00
   Sun (summer only) 12.00-18.00

FREE ✗ 🎁 ☂

I want to go here ☐

MAKE A CELTIC CROSS

...at the Brass Rubbing Centre

Despite what it might sound like, brass rubbing isn't about stroking metal! It's actually a form of art that was developed hundreds of years ago.

You get to choose what picture you want to 'rub' from a range of brass engravings. Most of them are medieval knights and their ladies, or symbols of the Picts and Celts (ancient Scottish tribespeople), such as the Celtic cross.

You select your colours and rub hard wax onto a piece of paper on top of the engraving. It's easy to get the hang of it and normal rubbings are about the size of this book. However, if you feel like a challenge you can attempt a rubbing of a life-size knight!

Sticker Scores

5	4	3
CELTIC CROSS	NOBLE KNIGHT	LIKEABLE LADY

2	1
PLEASANT PICT	CROSS CELT

WEST CENTRAL

EAST CENTRAL

NORTH

SOUTH & EAST

WEST

AROUND

TOP FIVES

Best Of The Rest

Just opposite the Brass Rubbing Centre is South Grays Close. The building used to be home to Scotland's Mint. This is the name for a place where money is printed – Scotland didn't have a building just to house an extra-fresh sweet!

Search for the engraving on nearby Heave Awa Hoose. A building collapsed here in the 1800s, killing 35 people. While rescuers were searching the rubble they heard a young boy shout, 'Heave away chaps, I'm no' dead yet!'. Look closely and you'll see the boy's words written above the arch at Paisley Close.

← It would take a while to rub all these!

How do you make a Celtic Cross? Stamp on his foot!

Fascinating Facts

★ The Brass Rubbing Centre is in a church called Trinity Apse. The church used to be part of Trinity College on a different site, but was demolished in the 1840s to make way for Waverley Train Station.

★ When Trinity Apse was moved, they numbered each stone to help them work out how to reconstruct it piece by piece, like a giant jigsaw puzzle. If you look closely you can still see the numbers engraved on some stones!

★ Memorial brasses were popular between 1200 and 1600 and were often found in churches. They usually featured important people or religious figures.

PLAN YOUR VISIT 19

The Brass Rubbing Centre

Trinity Apse, Chalmers Close, Royal Mile, EH1 1SS
www.edinburgh.gov.uk/museums

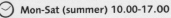

📞 0131 556 4364

🕐 Mon-Sat (summer) 10.00-17.00

£ ☂

I want to go here ☐

SEE A SECRET STAIRCASE

...at Holyrood Palace

Having your own secret staircase would be pretty cool. You could freak your family out by jumping from room to room. Unfortunately for Mary, Queen of Scots, having a secret passage was not so satisfying, because it was used to murder her favourite servant . . .

The stairway in question is in Holyrood Palace, which was Mary's home. When you visit you'll see the rooms she used to live in.

As you enter Mary's bedchamber, look to your left and hidden behind a tapestry you'll see the secret staircase. Mary's jealous husband used it to smuggle armed men into the room in order to kill David Rizzio, her secretary. Even now you can still see the blood spot from where he was stabbed. *Eww!*

Sticker Scores

5 — MARVELLOUS MANSION

4 — CHARMING CHATEAU

3 — PLEASANT PLACE

2 — CRUMBLING COTTAGE

1 — DOG HOUSE

WEST CENTRAL

EAST CENTRAL

NORTH

SOUTH & EAST

WEST

AROUND

TOP FIVES

Best Of The Rest

🔑 Look out for the portraits of kings in the Great Gallery. Some of them are not true likenesses of kings at all because the painter (Jacob de Wet) had no idea what they looked like!

🔑 Ask for one of the palace's activity trails, which will help you find the most fun things to look out for.

Top Tip
The palace is closed when the Queen is in residence so check whether she's in town before you visit! You can tell because her special flag, or standard, will be flying from the flagpole.

← Holyrood Palace

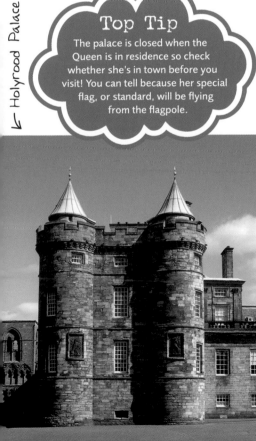

Fascinating Facts

⭐ Mary, Queen of Scots became queen when she was just six days old, after her dad died in 1542! Thankfully, she had a grown-up (known as a regent) to rule on her behalf until she became an adult. Presumably her first official royal orders were 'waaaaaah!!'.

⭐ Holyrood is the name for the Queen's park and palace. It has nothing to do with Hollywood, which is the part of Los Angeles where the American movie industry is based. So don't mix up Holyrood and Hollywood, or people will think you are *jolly rude*!

When is a piece of wood like the Queen? When it's a ruler.

PLAN YOUR VISIT 20
Palace of Holyroodhouse
Abbey Strand, Canongate, EH8 8DX
www.royalcollection.org.uk

📞 0131 556 5100

🕐 Daily (summer) 09:30-16:30
Daily (out of season) 09.30-18.00
Closed when royalty in residence.

££ 🍴 🎁 ☂

I want to go here ☐

RAMBLE DOWN A ROYAL ROUTE

...on the Royal Mile

Visitors to the Royal Mile today can ramble down it, enjoying the stroll. However, if you had been the King of Scotland you wouldn't have had to ramble. You would have been carried in a grand carriage!

The Royal Mile got its name from the King's regular journey between the castle (at the top of the Royal Mile) and his palace (at the bottom). As you wander down the King's route, imagine the hustle and bustle of old Edinburgh.

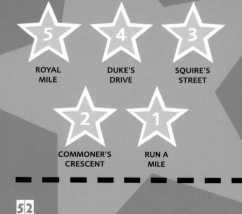

Sticker Scores

5 ROYAL MILE

4 DUKE'S DRIVE

3 SQUIRE'S STREET

2 COMMONER'S CRESCENT

1 RUN A MILE

Bear in mind that locals used to chuck their waste out of the windows as there were no toilets in the flats. So watch out for flying poo!

Best Of The Rest

🔑 Find the heart in the pavement outside St Giles Cathedral. It's called the Heart of Midlothian, and it marks the spot where the Tolbooth prison used to stand. One of Edinburgh's two main football teams is named after the heart.

🔑 Look out for the wellheads (the big square stones on the pavement) along the Royal Mile. Water was pumped here from the hills surrounding Edinburgh, and the locals used the wellheads to fill their barrels.

← Looking down the Royal Mile

Photo Op
Crowd into a close – one of the tiny alleys leading off the Royal Mile. Make sure the close name is in the pic with you.

Fascinating Facts

⭐ You may notice that the buildings along the Royal Mile are surprisingly tall. There's a good reason why. Old Edinburgh was often under threat of attack from the English, so they built a wall around the city. This meant that as the city grew bigger it had to go upwards and not outwards. And so Edinburgh got its own medieval skyscrapers!

⭐ Some people believe that if you spit on the Heart of Midlothian it will bring you good luck. Just make sure you don't try if someone is already standing on it!

PLAN YOUR VISIT 21

The Royal Mile
Castle Esplanade, Lawnmarket, High Street, Canongate

FREE

I want to go here ☐

WEST CENTRAL

EAST CENTRAL

NORTH

SOUTH & EAST

WEST

AROUND

TOP FIVES

CHECK OUT THE CHAMBER

...at the Scottish Parliament

Some people visit the Scottish Parliament building to see where politicians make decisions about the future of Scotland. Others just come because it's a really cool building!

Scotland had no parliament between 1707 and 1999, so when they got it back they were determined to make the new building look special. Unusual patterns are everywhere, such as leaves and upturned boat shapes. We particularly like the chamber, which has loads of oak beams sticking out of the ceiling.

You can take a guided tour on certain days, or reserve tickets to watch debates from the chamber's public gallery. However, check the schedule carefully when you book, or you might end up watching a long discussion about fishing policy!

Sticker Scores

5 FABULOUS FIRST MINISTER

4 POWERFUL POLITICIAN

3 SENSIBLE SECRETARY

2 SIMPLE SPEECHWRITER

1 RUBBISH RESEARCHER

WEST CENTRAL

EAST CENTRAL

NORTH

SOUTH & EAST

WEST

AROUND

TOP FIVES

Best Of The Rest

🔑 Marvel at the silver mace in the Parliament's foyer. If you look closely you'll see writing on it. Look out for where it says 'There shall be a Scottish Parliament'.

🔑 Check out the weird, sticky-out windows on the outside of the building. They are called Think Pods, and each one is a different politician's office. What do you think they look like?

🔑 Ask for a quiz about the Scottish Parliament at the information desk in the main hall.

← Where Scottish politicians make decisions

Fascinating Facts

★ Scotland is part of the United Kingdom of Great Britain and Northern Ireland. While some decisions are still made by the UK Parliament in London, since 1999 Scotland has also had a Parliament with powers of its own.

★ The Parliament building's unusual design has caused some headaches for Scotland's politicians. In 2005, one of the oak beams popped out from the ceiling and Parliament had to move elsewhere while it was fixed!

Top Tip

To see the Scottish Parliament in full swing, book tickets for First Minister's Questions. This is the most important session of the week, and it happens at 12.00 on Thursdays.

PLAN YOUR VISIT 22

The Scottish Parliament

EH99 1SP

www.scottish.parliament.uk

📞 0131 348 5200

🕐 **Mon-Sat: times vary.**
Book in advance for guided tours and chamber tickets.

FREE 🍽 🎁 ☂

I want to go here ☐

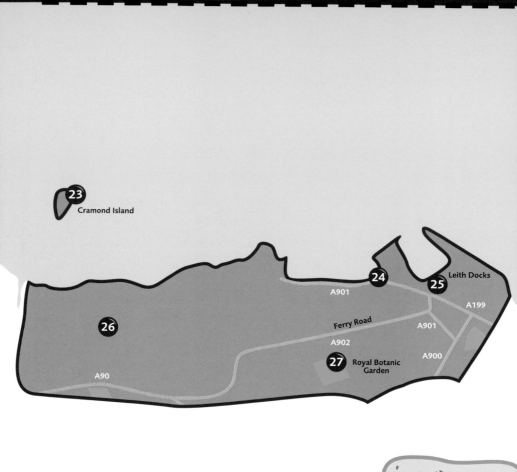

23 Cramond Island

24

25 Leith Docks

A901

A199

26

Ferry Road

A901

A902

27 Royal Botanic Garden

A900

A90

KEY

Places

Parks

H.M.Y BRITANNIA

WEST CENTRAL

EAST CENTRAL

NORTH

SOUTH & EAST

WEST

AROUND

TOP FIVES

WALK THROUGH THE WAVES

...to Cramond Island

Unless you have magical powers we would not normally recommend walking through the sea. However, it's a great way to get to Cramond Island – and if you follow our advice you won't even get wet!

Cramond Island is in the Firth of Forth, just north of Edinburgh. During World War Two it was an important military post where soldiers used to keep watch for enemy ships. You can still see the remains of military buildings, including an ammunition store, when you visit.

Start on the promenade at Cramond (a village on the mainland) and follow the paved path to reach the island. The walk takes about 20 minutes. Just make sure you get back to land before the tide turns or you'll be marooned!

Sticker Scores

5 TREASURE ISLAND

4 LEISURE ISLAND

3 DESERT ISLAND

2 TRAFFIC ISLAND

1 UNDER WATER

Similar Spots

 Take an island boat tour and see wildlife like puffins, cormorants and gannets. Forth Boat Tours run various trips from Queensferry. (Sadly the water's too deep to walk!)

Top Tip
Check the tide times carefully before you go so that you don't get stranded. The crossing can only be completed a maximum of two hours before and after low tide.

What do you get if you cross a rabbit and a shellfish? The *Oyster* Bunny!

← The way to Cramond Island

Fascinating Facts

★ Cramond village was the site of a Roman fort, so it's quite likely the Romans used to enjoy *roamin'* around Cramond Island too!

★ The island was also used for sheep farming, and you can still see the remains of an old farm building in the centre of the island. It must have been a lonely place – presumably the farmers that lived on Cramond Island were too *sheep*-ish to move to the mainland!

★ There are more than a dozen islands in the Firth of Forth. Several of them were home to monks and hermits who liked the peaceful surroundings. One was even used as a prison. We're guessing the inmates were not so enthusiastic about isolated island living!

PLAN YOUR VISIT 23

Cramond Island
Off Cramond, EH4

FREE

I want to go here ☐

WEST CENTRAL

EAST CENTRAL

NORTH

SOUTH & EAST

WEST

AROUND

TOP FIVES

CLIMB IN A CHURCH

...at Alien Rock

Despite the name, Alien Rock is not a stone stolen from extra-terrestrials. But you will get slightly closer to outer space if you make it to the top of this indoor climbing centre!

Alien Rock is a climbing centre built in an old church. It's a great place for experts and first time climbers alike.

When you arrive you are given a harness and boots. You then choose a wall and make your way upwards using the hand and foot holds. Don't worry about falling - you're attached to a safety rope at all times. Beginners aged eight and over should check out the weekly Kids Club on Saturdays and Sundays. It's the perfect way to learn how to become a cracking climber!

Sticker Scores

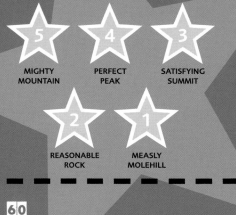

5 MIGHTY MOUNTAIN

4 PERFECT PEAK

3 SATISFYING SUMMIT

2 REASONABLE ROCK

1 MEASLY MOLEHILL

WEST CENTRAL

EAST CENTRAL

NORTH

SOUTH & EAST

WEST

AROUND

TOP FIVES

Similar Spots

Tackle an aerial assault course at the Edinburgh International Climbing Arena in Ratho. You climb up ropes and over planks which are up to 30 metres in the air. That's as tall as twenty eleven year old kids standing on each other's shoulders (but much less wobbly)!
www.eica-ratho.com

Climb sideways at nearby Alien Rock 2. The twist here is that you don't use ropes and you climb across rather than upwards!

← Unlike any church you've seen before

Fascinating Facts

★ Perhaps the most famous climber in the world was Sir Edmund Hillary. In 1953 he became the first person known to have reached the summit of Mount Everest. At 8,848 metres above sea level that's the same height as around 800 Alien Rock climbing walls. Now that's really *summit*!

★ There is a climbing wall in Sweden that plays a musical note as you touch each hold. Sounds great!

Top Tip

If you haven't climbed before, and if your grown-ups don't know how to climb, you should book an instructor to *show you the ropes*!

PLAN YOUR VISIT 24

Alien Rock 1

8 Pier Place, EH6 4LP

www.alienrock.co.uk

📞 0131 552 7211

🕐 Mon-Fri 11.00-22.00
Sat-Sun 10.00-19.00
Kids club: Sat-Sun 10.00-12.00 or 13.00-15.00

I want to go here ☐

SEE THE QUEEN'S BOAT

...at the HMY Britannia

The Queen has lots of cool stuff: a private army, plenty of palaces and of course the crown jewels. And, on top of all that, until 1997 she also had her very own royal yacht!

Her Majesty's Yacht *Britannia* is a huge luxury yacht that was launched in 1953. It was the 83rd royal yacht and was used by Queen Elizabeth to travel to meet important people all around the world.

Onboard you can see exactly how the Royal Family would have lived during these trips.

H.M.Y BRITANNIA

Sticker Scores

5 QUEEN'S QUARTERS

4 CAPTAIN'S CABIN

3 SEA HAND'S HAMMOCK

2 CABIN BOY'S COUCH

1 STOWAWAY'S SLEEPING BAG

It has an operating theatre for medical emergencies, a garage complete with a Rolls Royce and even a special post office (although we're not sure how the postman delivered letters to the middle of the ocean!).

Best Of The Rest

🔑 Hang out at the Ocean Terminal arcade, beside *Britannia*'s mooring post. As well as loads of shops, there's a cinema, a play centre and even an indoor skate park!

Photo Op
Wave like the Queen from the ship's bow to your adoring public on the shore.

Who held the baby octopus for ransom? *Squid*-nappers!

← Aboard the HMY Britannia

Fascinating Facts

⭐ **King Charles II started the trend for royal yachts when he commissioned the HMY *Queen Mary* in 1660. He liked it so much he went on to collect 25 of them, making his yearning for yachts a rather expensive hobby . . .**

⭐ Unlike most crews, sailors on the *Britannia* were forbidden from shouting orders. Instead they had to use hand signals so they didn't disturb the resting royals!

⭐ **The Queen really wanted a coal fire in the drawing room but was told that, for fire safety reasons, a crewman would have to stand beside with a bucket of water at all times. So she went for an electric one instead.**

PLAN YOUR VISIT 25

The Royal Yacht Britannia
Ocean Terminal, Leith, EH6 6JJ
www.royalyachtbritannia.co.uk

📞 0131 555 5566

🕐 Daily (summer) 09.30-17.30
Daily (out of season) 10.00-16.30

££ ✖

I want to go here ☐

WEST CENTRAL
EAST CENTRAL
NORTH
SOUTH & EAST
WEST
AROUND
TOP FIVES

HUNT FOR A HIDDEN HALLWAY

...at Lauriston Castle

Most houses would be happy to have one hidden passage. However, Lauriston Castle has two! See if you can find them both . . .

The oldest parts of Lauriston Castle were built over 400 years ago. Successive owners updated it, and by 1902 it was an impressively modern home, with electricity, running water and even central heating. But of course, you're not visiting to inspect the plumbing. You're there to hunt for hidden passages!

The first secret passage is hidden behind a shutter in the study and leads to a tiny hallway room. The second one is in the library and leads down a staircase to a back door. Once you've found them, think what you'd use them for if you lived there!

Sticker Scores

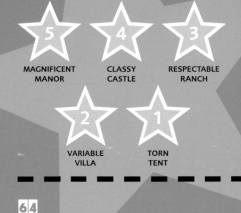

★ 5	★ 4	★ 3
MAGNIFICENT MANOR	CLASSY CASTLE	RESPECTABLE RANCH

★ 2	★ 1
VARIABLE VILLA	TORN TENT

Similar Spots

🔑 Check out Dalmeny House, another grand home which overlooks the Firth of Forth. The house's collection includes a weird mechanical dice game from 1737.

🔑 Alternatively, take an outdoor nature trail at Hopetoun House, another superb stately home. The grounds cover 150 acres and contain all kinds of animals, including delightful deer, fantastic frogs and pleasant pheasants.

Top Tip
Lauriston Castle grounds are a great place for a picnic during the summer.

← In the grounds of Lauriston Castle

Fascinating Facts

⭐ **Girls and boys were sometimes hard to tell apart in Britain in 1902. Look out for the picture of a little boy with long curly hair in a dress at Lauriston Castle. It is an early portrait of the future King Edward!**

⭐ Secret passages have been around for a long time. Some Egyptian pyramids had hidden corridors to help guard the burial chambers – and they are over 4,000 years old!

⭐ **The penthouse suite at the Fairmont Hotel in San Francisco contains a secret passage hidden behind a bookcase! Mind you, it costs $10,000 per night to stay there, so we think you're better off visiting Lauriston Castle instead . . .**

PLAN YOUR VISIT 26

Lauriston Castle

2A Cramond Road South, Davidson's Mains, EH4 5QD

www.edinburgh.gov.uk/museums

📞 0131 336 2060

🕐 Sat-Thu (summer) daily tours at 14.00
Sat-Sun (winter) daily tours at 14.00

I want to go here ☐

WEST CENTRAL

EAST CENTRAL

NORTH

SOUTH & EAST

WEST

AROUND

TOP FIVES

CHECK WHERE CHOCOLATE COMES FROM

...at the Royal Botanic Gardens

Have you ever wished that chocolate grew on trees? Well, at the Botanic Gardens it does – sort of. In the glasshouses you'll find the main ingredients of chocolate.

The Royal Botanic Gardens are home to thousands of plants from around the world. The collections include incredible orchids, tall trees and water lilies that look like tea trays!

Make sure you include a tour of the glasshouses, which are heated to various different temperatures so that plants from around the world can survive.

Sticker Scores

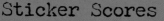

5	4	3
CRACKING COCOA	LOVELY LILY	TERRIFIC TREE

2	1
PASSABLE PLANT	COMPOST HEAP

Look out for the sugar and cocoa plants in the Plants & People glasshouse. Just don't lick the leaves – they won't taste like a Mars bar!

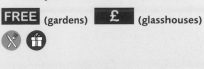

Best Of The Rest

🔑 The Montane Tropics glasshouse contains a collection of carnivorous plants, such as the venus flytrap. These are flowers that feed on real, living creatures! So watch your fingers . . .

🔑 The Plants & People glasshouse contains giant Victoria lilies, which are shaped like huge, green tea trays.

🔑 Look out for the spectacular, summer-flowering handkerchief tree in the Arboretum. It's not to be *sneezed* at!

← Where chocolate comes from

Fascinating Facts

⭐ One of the glasshouses – the Temperate Palm House – is the tallest of its kind in the world. It's as high as five double decker buses (but less likely to give you a lift to the shops).

⭐ Carnivorous plants use cunning techniques to catch their food. Fly-paper traps are covered in a gluey gunk so that insects stick to the leaves. Snap traps (such as the venus flytrap) have leaves that can close rapidly around their prey. However, they generally only eat insects and spiders – they would struggle with a burger and fries!

Top Tip
Get an audio guide to zoom you round the glasshouses. It's the easiest way to work out what you're looking at.

PLAN YOUR VISIT 27

Royal Botanic Garden Edinburgh
20A Inverleith Row, EH3 5LR
www.rbge.org.uk

📞 0131 248 2901

🕐 Daily (summer) 10.00-19.00
Daily (out of season) 10.00-16.00

FREE (gardens) £ (glasshouses)

🍴 🎁

I want to go here ☐

WEST CENTRAL
EAST CENTRAL
NORTH
SOUTH & EAST
WEST
AROUND
TOP FIVES

SOUTH & EAST

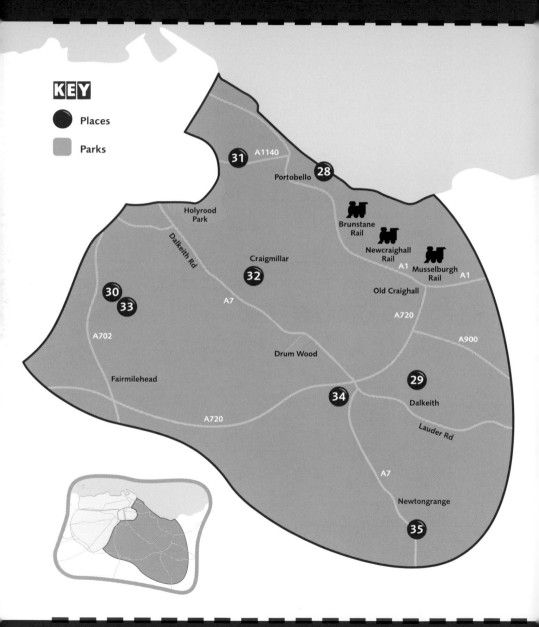

KEY

● Places

Parks

31 A1140

28 Portobello

Holyrood Park

Dalkeith Rd

Brunstane Rail

Newcraighall Rail

Craigmillar

32

Musselburgh Rail

A1

A1

Old Craighall

30 33

A7

A720

A702

A900

Drum Wood

Fairmilehead

34

29

Dalkeith

A720

Lauder Rd

A7

Newtongrange

35

WEST CENTRAL

EAST CENTRAL

NORTH

SOUTH & EAST

WEST

AROUND

TOP FIVES

BUILD A SANDCASTLE

...at Portobello Beach

Many people come to Edinburgh without realising that there's a great beach on their doorstep. Portobello is just a few miles from the city centre – and it's the perfect place for building sandcastles!

Portobello is known as Edinburgh's seaside. The beach is one of Scotland's cleanest, and there are also play parks and arcades to visit along the shore. The sand is great for building things and burying family members – just make sure you ask permission first!

For a real sandcastle challenge, try adding a moat or a tunnel without your castle collapsing. You could even try to make it look like the real Edinburgh Castle!

Sticker Scores

5 BRILLIANT BEACH

4 SUPER SEASIDE

3 COOL COAST

2 SATISFACTORY SHORE

1 SINKING SAND

Best Of The Rest

🔑 Wander around the amusement arcades on the promenade or check out the nearby play park.

🔑 If you don't fancy swimming in the sea then why not take a dip in the Turkish baths at Portobello Swim Centre (see p127). You can try the three rooms at different temperatures before cooling off in the Frigidarium.

Top Tip

If you fancy a picnic but want to keep sand out of your sandwiches, go and eat on one of the grassy areas just off the beach.

↙ Portobello Beach

Fascinating Facts

⭐ **During the 1700s, Portobello beach was a favourite haunt for smugglers. They brought valuable goods such as salt, tea and tobacco into Edinburgh under the cover of night in order to avoid paying taxes.**

⭐ The Portobello Beach area used to be called Figgate Muir. This might sound like an unpleasant pudding, but it's actually the old English for 'cow's ditch'. It got this name because monks used to keep animals on the moorland near the beach.

⭐ **The beach was renamed Portobello by a sailor after a battle he'd fought in Central America. The British victory at Portobello, Panama was celebrated throughout the country and many places were named after it.**

PLAN YOUR VISIT 28

Portobello Beach
Bellfield Street, EH15

📞 0131 657 4990

FREE

I want to go here ☐

71

DROP DOWN A DEATH SLIDE

...at Dalkeith Country Estate

Don't worry, this slide won't really lead you to your death! Death slides are steep slides which make you feel like you're dropping to your doom. And the one at Dalkeith is dead good!

Dalkeith Country Estate is a brilliant place to burn off some energy. You can cycle in the grounds or book a barbecue pit so that you and your family can chomp on some burnt meat!

The main attraction, however, is the awesome adventure playground.

Sticker Scores

5 FLYING FOX

4 SUPER SLIDE

3 RESPECTABLE RUNWAY

2 SLIGHT SLOPE

1 STANDING STILL

As well as the usual rope bridges and tyre swings there is an amazing death slide, and an intense aerial runway, called the flying fox. Climb to the top, then hold on tight before zooming down the death-defying zip wire.

WEST CENTRAL

EAST CENTRAL

NORTH

SOUTH & EAST

WEST

AROUND

TOP FIVES

Best Of The Rest

🔑 Wander along the tree-top walkway. Head to the fortress and see if you can capture the flag.

🔑 Hide in the park's cave. Just don't stay hidden for long or the grown-ups might go home without you!

🔑 Take a walk along a nature trail. You could see otters, badgers and deer in the grounds of the estate.

Similar Spots

🔑 Nearby Vogrie Country Park also has a great adventure playground, as well as a miniature railway and a short golf course.

← Dalkeith Country Park

Fascinating Facts

★ Dalkeith House is built on the site of an old castle. It has a dungeon and a torture chamber, so it was clearly not a good idea to get on the wrong side of the original owner!

★ During World War Two the estate was the base for a whole division of tanks! Sadly you're unlikely to find any armoured vehicles in the estate's car park today . . .

★ Europe's longest aerial runway is in Newquay, Cornwall. It's 750 metres long – which is almost as long as two circuits of an Olympic running track (or over 1,000 foxes lying end to end).

Photo Op
Take a picture of you on your favourite bit of the awesome adventure playground!

PLAN YOUR VISIT

Dalkeith Country Estate
Dalkeith, EH22 2NJ
www.dalkeithcountryestate.com

📞 0131 654 1666

🕐 **Daily (summer) 10.00-17.30**

£ ✕

I want to go here ☐

SEE THE COUNTRYSIDE IN THE CITY

...at the Hermitage of Braid

It's not often you can't see any buildings or hear any cars while in the city. But it's possible at the Hermitage of Braid – a quiet valley a few miles south of the centre of Edinburgh.

The Hermitage of Braid is a nature reserve packed with foxes, otters and all kinds of birds. A long time ago the valley was full of ice, but now it's a great place for a stroll.

Wander along the Braid Burn and listen out for the distinctive, drumming sound of the great spotted woodpecker.

COUNTRY
0 MILES

CITY
0 MILES

Keep a look out for dippers, herons and kingfishers too. Then head to Blackford pond where you could find swans, geese and coots. You'd have to be a *bird-brain* not to go!

Sticker Scores

5 WONDERFUL WALK

4 AWESOME AMBLE

3 STEADY STROLL

2 MEDIOCRE MARCH

1 HORRIBLE HIKE

Best Of The Rest

🔑 Check out the Ice House, which was built in the 1700s.

🔑 Look for the old doocot, a house for pigeons or doves. The birds that used to live here would have been farmed for their meat.

🔑 Drop in to the visitor centre to find out about the history of the park and its wildlife.

← Trees in the middle of the city

Photo Op
Climb from Hermitage House to the top of Blackford Hill and you'll see one of the best views of Edinburgh.

Fascinating Facts

★ Sadly, an ice house isn't a house made of ice (that's an igloo). Instead it's a place where ice was stored in the days before refrigerators.

★ The name Braid probably came from the De Brad family, who lived in the area from the 1100s to the 1300s. It has nothing to do with hair braids (though nobody will stop you wearing your hair in plaits when you visit if you really want to)!

Top Tip
The website of the Royal Society for the Protection of Birds (www.rspb.org.uk) contains audio clips of the call of every imaginable bird. Search before you visit so you'll recognise the sound of dippers, herons, kingfishers and woodpeckers.

PLAN YOUR VISIT 30

The Hermitage of Braid

69a Braid Road, EH10 6JF

www.edinburgh.gov.uk/countrysiderangers

📞 0131 447 7145

🕐 Park open 24 hours

FREE

I want to go here ☐

WEST CENTRAL
EAST CENTRAL
NORTH
SOUTH & EAST
WEST
AROUND
TOP FIVES

LASER A LOVED ONE

...at Dark Ocean

There are not very many occasions in life where it is acceptable for you to shoot a chum with a laser gun. However, it's actually encouraged when you're taking part in this ocean-themed laser game!

Dark Ocean is a laser gaming venue. You can play games where you shoot at everyone, play as a team, or attempt to complete specific missions.

It's a bit like being inside a real life computer game – you'll find hidden gems around the arena that give you special powers!

Sticker Scores

5	**4**	**3**
HOT SHOT	MARVELLOUS MARKSMAN	SEASONED SOLDIER
2	**1**	
GRUMBLING GAMER	LONG SHOT	

Look out for the rapid fire, invincibility and (our favourite!) invisibility bonuses . . . So dive into the deep and train your trigger finger for some laser action!

Similar Spots

🔑 For some more laser fun, head to the zap-tastic Laser Quest near Haymarket rail station.
www.laserquest-edinburgh.co.uk

🔑 If you're a fan of computer games, look out for the Edinburgh Interactive Festival every August. Have a go on the interactive exhibits, or attend one of the free screenings of new games.
www.edinburghinteractive.co.uk

← Ready, aim, fire!

Top Tip
When you hear Dark Ocean's countdown timer go off, get out of the way. As quickly as you can. Really.

Fascinating Facts

⭐ **Laser games do not actually use real lasers. They use invisible technology called infrared, which is the same thing that makes a TV remote control work. So don't point your laser gun at a telly or you might accidentally change the channel!**

⭐ Laser is an acronym (a word where each of the letters stands for another word) of Light Amplification by the Stimulated Emission of Radiation. However, that's a bit of a tongue-twister, so usually people just say laser.

⭐ **Scientists believe they may be able to make a real life invisibility cloak. In 2010 the Science journal described a device that could bend light to hide an object. Now that _would_ be handy when you fancy a midnight snack!**

PLAN YOUR VISIT 31

Dark Ocean
46a Portobello Road, EH8 7EL
www.darkocean.co.uk

📞 0131 661 4650

🕐 Daily 11.00-22.00

£

I want to go here ☐

WEST CENTRAL

EAST CENTRAL

NORTH

SOUTH & EAST

WEST

AROUND

TOP FIVES

CLAMBER OVER A CASTLE

...at Craigmillar Castle

Some castles rope off the interesting bits, but at Craigmillar you can explore every nook and cranny. Just don't get locked in the dungeon!

Craigmillar Castle was built over 500 years ago and is one of the coolest castles in Scotland. New owners kept adding bits on, so it's really more like several castles rolled into one.

Climb up onto the top of the battlements and imagine an enemy army advancing. Or, if you want to feel like an old Scottish warrior, why not buy a bow and arrow from the visitor centre? Just make sure you don't fire at unsuspecting tourists!

Sticker Scores

5 CRACKING CASTLE

4 FEARSOME FORTRESS

3 SECURE STRONGHOLD

2 CRUMBLING KEEP

1 SANDCASTLE

Best Of The Rest

🔑 Visit the P-shaped fish pond in the grounds of the castle. The P stands for Preston, which is the surname of the castle's original owners.

🔑 Stand among pigeons in the dovecot. Though people have not lived at Craigmillar Castle for hundreds of years, the pigeons still think it's a perfectly decent home!

Photo Op
Get a snap of you on top of the battlements. Pose as if you're defending the castle from invaders!

← Craigmillar Castle

Fascinating Facts

⭐ The castle was abandoned in the early 1700s because the owners wanted to live somewhere more comfortable. You may think it sounds cool to live in a castle, but for them it was just downright cold!

⭐ Confusingly, the word dovecot means a house for doves or pigeons. Presumably people thought that pigeoncot didn't sound as good. There's also one at the Hermitage of Braid (see p74)

⭐ Pigeons and doves are part of the same bird family. Doves are slightly smaller, and both animals are very adaptable. They can live just about anywhere in the world, except for the desert.

PLAN YOUR VISIT 32

Craigmillar Castle
Craigmillar Castle Road, EH16 4SY
www.historic-scotland.gov.uk

📞 0131 661 4445

🕐 Daily (summer) 09.30-17.30
Sat-Wed (out of season) 09.30-16.30

£

I want to go here ☐

WEST CENTRAL
EAST CENTRAL
NORTH
SOUTH & EAST
WEST
AROUND
TOP FIVES

HIT A HOLE IN ONE

...at the Hermitage Family Golf Course

Golf sometimes has a reputation as a sport for boring old men. That's partly because lots of golf clubs are full of boring old men. Thankfully, this place is designed with kids in mind!

The Hermitage Family Golf Course was created specifically for families. It is shorter than an adult course and cheaper too. There are twelve holes in total: six easier ones and six that are a bit harder. So you should be able to enjoy bashing a ball around even if you've never played before. Clubs can be hired from the reception if you don't have any of your own. So get down there and try to hit a birdie!

Sticker Scores

5 AMAZING ALBATROSS

4 EXCELLENT EAGLE

3 BRAVE BIRDIE

2 PASSABLE PAR

1 BIG BOGEY

WEST CENTRAL

EAST CENTRAL

NORTH

SOUTH & EAST

WEST

AROUND

TOP FIVES

Similar Spots

 Princes golf course, next to the Hermitage course, is aimed at twelve to eighteen year olds. There's also a driving range beside it. (That's a place for practising your golf swing – NOT a place to bring your car!)

There is a free pitch and putt golf course on The Meadows in the summer, just south of the centre (see p124). Non-golfers can kick a ball about or play Frisbee in the park.

Why did the golfer wear two pairs of socks?

In case he got a hole in one!

← Go golfing

Fascinating Facts

★ The scoring system for golf is rather confusing. Each hole has a set number of shots that you are expected to take, called the par. If you score one less than par, you get a birdie. If you score one more, you get a bogey. (Obviously that's just what your score is called – nobody actually gives you a bird or some snot!)

★ Tiger Woods, an American golfer, hit his first hole in one at the age of eight. Mind you, he didn't have to play with a wild Edinburgh wind swirling around him!

★ Golf balls used to be made from feathers! The Scots who started the game used to stuff leather pouches with boiled feathers.

PLAN YOUR VISIT 33

Hermitage Family Golf Course

11 Braids Hill Drive, EH10 6GZ

✆ 0131 447 5700

££

I want to go here ☐

SPOT A STICK INSECT

...at Butterfly and Insect World

Butterflies and insects may be small, but they are the kings and queens of camouflage! At Butterfly and Insect World, you'll see how some have evolved to blend in with nature . . .

Take a tour of the tropical rainforest and keep your eyes peeled for twigs that twitch and leaves that lurch. The helpful staff will point these hidden creatures out to you if you're struggling to see them.

Stick insects are particularly tricky to spot – their branch-like bodies help them to stay out of sight of predators and avoid coming to a *stick*-y end! Look out also for the glass-winged butterfly which blends in with its background, and the owl butterfly which frightens foes with its owl-eyed wings.

Sticker Scores

⭐ **5** FLYING HIGH

⭐ **4** SOARING SWEETLY

⭐ **3** GLIDING GENTLY

⭐ **2** ATTEMPTING TAKE-OFF

⭐ **1** GOBBLED UP

Best Of The Rest

🔑 **Pick up pythons, tarantulas and millipedes** at one of the animal handling sessions at 12.00 and 15.00.

🔑 **Gawp at glowing scorpions** in the Nocturnal Zone.

🔑 **Behave at the beehive,** or you might get stung!

Photo Op
Scare your friends with a picture of you touching a tarantula or stroking a snake!

What do insects learn at school?
Moth-matics!

← An owl butterfly

Fascinating Facts

⭐ **Stick insects often rock from side to side. This is not because they're listening to a tiny iPod – it's so that they look even more like sticks and leaves blowing in the wind.**

⭐ Stick insects are popular pets as they're easy to look after and can be kept in fairly small containers, such as a jar with a few holes in the top.

⭐ **Butterflies taste with their feet! They flit from flower to flower, looking for tasty nectar. So if they land on you, it's probably because they think you're a giant flower.**

⭐ You might think that butterflies are soft and friendly creatures. Actually, they can get pretty aggressive. Look out for butterflies with ripped wings: they're the ones who lost out in a butterfly battle!

PLAN YOUR VISIT 34
Butterfly and Insect World
Dobbies Garden World, Melville Nursery, Lasswade, Midlothian, EH18 1AZ
www.edinburgh-butterfly-world.co.uk

📞 **0131 663 4932**

🕐 **Daily (summer) 09.30-17.30**
Daily (out of season) 10.00-17.00

 ❌ 🎁

I want to go here ☐

WEST CENTRAL

EAST CENTRAL

NORTH

SOUTH & EAST

WEST

AROUND

TOP FIVES

GO DOWN THE PIT

...at the Scottish Mining Museum

At the Scottish Mining Museum, you see what life was like working in a cramped, dark and cold pit. Just be glad you weren't born a couple of hundred years ago – in the 1800s children as young as five worked down the mines!

Coal mining used to be really important to Scotland's economy – but it was not an easy job. During your visit you'll get a sense of the tough conditions the miners worked in. Fortunately the staff at the Scottish Mining Museum just want to show you what the mine was like, not make you work down there.

Choose to take a guided tour, or put on a helmet (complete with headphones and a built-in audio tour) to walk around at your own pace. *It's the pits* . . . in a good way!

Sticker Scores

5 MASSIVE MINE

4 CRAMPED COALFACE

3 ORDINARY OIL WELL

2 QUESTIONABLE QUARRY

1 THE PITS

WEST CENTRAL

EAST CENTRAL

NORTH

SOUTH & EAST

WEST

AROUND

TOP FIVES

Best Of The Rest

🔑 Squeeze through a tight tunnel in A Race Apart, the interactive exhibition. You'll find out if you would have made it as a miner!

🔑 Build a bridge, find out about friction and learn about levers in the hands-on Operation Centre.

← Mine how you go!

Photo Op

Get a snap of you taken working the winding engine. Make sure the men and coal get to the bottom of the shaft safely.

Top Tip

Visit on Wednesday or Sunday and you can take the Big Stuff tour of the museum's massive mining machinery.

Fascinating Facts

★ Entire families used to work down the mine. In 1842 women, girls and boys under ten were banned from working there, but older boys were still able to work in the mine instead of going to school!

★ To prevent accidents, any miner found carrying a match would lose his job. A single spark could cause a huge explosion.

★ Carbon monoxide is a deadly gas that formed in coal mines. It's hard to detect, so miners took canaries down with them. If the bird passed out, that meant it had probably breathed in too much dangerous gas, and the miners would get out sharpish!

PLAN YOUR VISIT 35

Scottish Mining Museum
Lady Victoria Colliery, Newtongrange, EH22 4NQ
www.scottishminingmuseum.com

📞 0131 663 7519

🕐 Daily 10.00-16.00 (last tour at 14.30)

I want to go here ☐

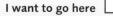

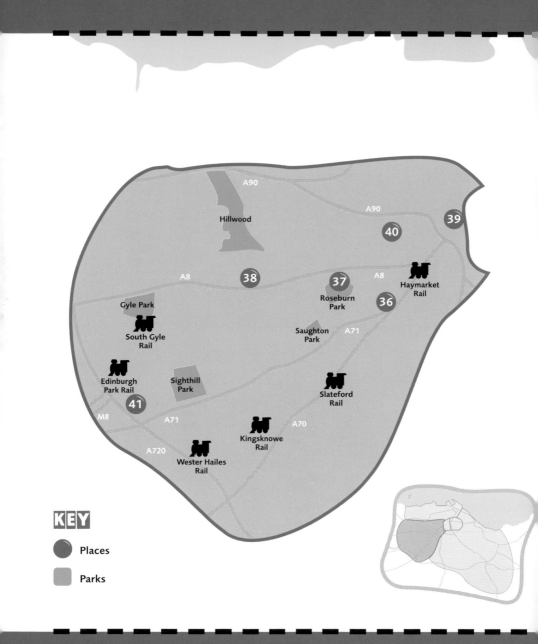

A90

A90

Hillwood

39

40

A8

38

A8

37

Haymarket
Rail

Roseburn
Park

36

Gyle Park

South Gyle
Rail

Saughton
Park

A71

Edinburgh
Park Rail

Sighthill
Park

Slateford
Rail

41

M8

A71

A70

Kingsknowe
Rail

A720

Wester Hailes
Rail

KEY

● Places

■ Parks

WEST CENTRAL

EAST CENTRAL

NORTH

SOUTH & EAST

WEST

AROUND

TOP FIVES

CUDDLE A CHICKEN

...at Gorgie City Farm

An old rubbish dump might not sound like the best place to put a farm, but that's what used to be here before Gorgie City Farm opened. Nowadays you'll find all sorts of animals, including cows, horses, pigs, sheep and an owl!

The farm would be worth visiting just to admire the animals, but there are plenty of special activities laid on too. Animal feeding, pony rides and lamb-walking are all offered regularly. There's also an old tractor near the play park which you can climb on.

Our favourite part is Cuddle Corner. This is a special bit of the farm where you can touch tortoises, ruffle rabbits, grasp guinea pigs and even cuddle a chicken! It's *gorgie*-ous!

Sticker Scores

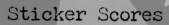

5 THRILLED TORTOISE

4 DELIGHTED DONKEY

3 HAPPY HEDGEHOG

2 CONTENTED COW

1 SAD SHEEP

Best Of The Rest

🔑 Look out for Bunty the cow. If you look closely you'll see that her tongue is huge, black and sticky. This is because she uses it like an elephant's trunk to grab grass from the ground and pull it into her mouth.

🔑 Sign up to do real farm jobs like mucking out the stables or collecting eggs. Farmers' Helpers sessions are available to kids aged eight to twelve during the school holidays. These must be booked in advance.

🔑 Join Gorgie City Farm's Young Farmer's Club. It meets once a month during school term time and is for eight to twelve year olds.

← Egg-cellent!

Fascinating Facts

⭐ Not all chicken eggs are yellow – the Ameraucana and Araucana chicken breeds lay blue and green eggs! It's quite *eggs*-traordinary!

Top Tip
The farm's activity schedule changes regularly so check the website or call ahead to find out what's on. Cuddle Corner runs on some Saturdays throughout the year.

What do you get when you cross a parrot with a centipede?
A Walkie-talkie!

PLAN YOUR VISIT 36

Gorgie City Farm
51 Gorgie Road, EH11 2LA
www.gorgiecityfarm.org.uk

📞 0131 337 4202

🕐 Daily (summer) 09.30-16.30
Daily (out of season) 09.30-16.00

FREE (donations welcomed) 🍴 🎁

I want to go here ☐

WEST CENTRAL

EAST CENTRAL

NORTH

SOUTH & EAST

WEST

AROUND

TOP FIVES

SKATE IN THE SHADOW OF A STADIUM

...at Murrayfield Ice Rink

Edinburgh used to be so cold that people would skate on the surface of ponds and rivers. It's still not exactly a tropical city, but sadly the wet bits don't freeze over any more.

However, you can always head to Murrayfield Ice Rink for some satisfying skating. The rink is right next to Murrayfield rugby stadium, so you can admire the famous venue as you go in.

Check the website for details of family sessions. There's even a special disco slot for rhythmic skaters! So strap on your skates and see if you can survive the slippery surface without slamming into someone. N-*ice*!

Sticker Scores

5	4	3
ICE CREAM	ICEBERG	ICE STORM

2	1
ICE CUBE	I SCREAM

WEST CENTRAL

EAST CENTRAL

NORTH

SOUTH & EAST

WEST

AROUND

TOP FIVES

Best Of The Rest

🔑 Watch ice hockey by attending an Edinburgh Capitals game. Murrayfield Ice Rink is home to the team, who play in the UK's Elite Ice Hockey League.

Photo Op

Get a snap of you gliding along on the ice. Or, if you're still learning, hold on to the rail, but cut your hand out of the photo so it looks like you're gliding effortlessly!

What is an ig?
A snow house without a loo!

Fascinating Facts

⭐ Ice hockey is similar to field hockey, but is played using a puck (a round disc that looks like a giant plastic penny) instead of a ball. The other main differences are that the players are on ice, not grass, and they're allowed to bash into each other.

⭐ The Olympic sport of curling started in Scotland and is played regularly at the ice rink. It involves pushing 'stones' across ice towards a target and it used to be played on frozen ponds.

Top Tip

Wrap up warm on the rink, and remember to take gloves and a hat. It's best to avoid wearing jeans because if they get wet they stay wet!

← Pigeons can ice skate too!

PLAN YOUR VISIT 37

Murrayfield Ice Rink
Riversdale Crescent, EH12 5XN
www.murrayfieldicerinkltd.co.uk

📞 0131 337 6933

🕐 Mon-Fri 14.30-19.00 or 21.00,
Sat 10.00-22.00, Sun 10.15-16.30
Session types vary, check before you visit.

I want to go here ☐

PEER AT A PENGUIN

...at Edinburgh Zoo

We're not talking about peering at *Club Penguin* on your computer! At Edinburgh Zoo you can see real penguins up close . . .

Edinburgh Zoo is home to hundreds of species, from lemurs to leopards to lorikeets. You can plan which ones you want to see in advance by checking out the kids' zone on the zoo's website.

Our favourites are the perfectly polite penguins. Each day there is a Penguin Parade, when the birds are allowed to wander around among the visitors. It's been taking place for 60 years, ever since a zookeeper accidentally let the penguins out. Just a warning though – the penguin area pongs of a mixture of fish and penguin poo, so you might need to hold your nose!

Sticker Scores

5 PERFECT PENGUIN

4 LOVELY LORIKEET

3 LIKEABLE LEOPARD

2 RUDE RHINO

1 HUNGRY HIPPO

WEST CENTRAL

EAST CENTRAL

NORTH

SOUTH & EAST

WEST

AROUND

TOP FIVES

Best Of The Rest

🔑 Become a parrot perch in the Rainbow Landings area. Rainbow lorikeets will land on your head as you walk through!

🔑 Check out the chimps on the Budongo Trail.

🔑 Admire the cute koalas in the Australian exhibit. They're the only koalas to be found in a zoo in the UK!

🔑 Or, if you fancy a break from the animals, clamber around on the zoo's climbing frame.

Top Tip
The zoo is on a hill, but you can avoid the trek to the top by taking the Hilltop Safari bus.

← Penguins on parade

Fascinating Facts

⭐ Edinburgh Zoo is home to a penguin that is also Colonel-in-Chief of the Norwegian King's Guard! Sir Nils Olav, the penguin in question, was adopted as a mascot by the King of Norway's marching band in 1972, and was later awarded a knighthood. So now Olav is a loyal royal penguin!

⭐ There are three kinds of penguin at Edinburgh Zoo: King, Gentoo and Rockhopper. King are the biggest and have yellow markings, whilst Gentoos are the fastest swimming bird in the world. They can reach speeds of around 25 miles per hour, which is over five times quicker than the fastest humans can swim!

PLAN YOUR VISIT 38

Edinburgh Zoo
134 Corstorphine Road, EH12 6TS
www.edinburghzoo.org.uk

📞 0131 334 9171

🕐 Daily (summer) 09.00-18.00
Daily (out of season) 09.00-16.30

£££ ✕ 🎁

I want to go here ☐

CHECK OUT THE CHILDREN'S GAMES

...at the Georgian House

250 years ago, children were supposed to be seen and not heard. If you were lucky, you were sometimes allowed into the parlour to play games. If you were unlucky, you had to work as a chimney sweep!

At the Georgian House you can play with traditional toys made from string and wood. For example, there's the cup and ball where you had to, *umm*, get a ball into a cup. Then there's the spinning top where you had to, *well*, make a top spin.

Now, we know these games may not sound as exciting as a Wii, but trust us they are addictive and require a good deal of patience and skill. See if you can beat the grown-ups!

Sticker Scores

5	4	3
SPINNING TOP	CUP AND BALL	DOLL'S HOUSE

2	1
NINTENDO Wii	ACTUAL WEE

Best Of The Rest

🔑 **Dress like a duke** during the school holidays by trying on some Georgian clothes in the activity room.

🔑 **See what life was like below stairs** for the servants and maids in the house's kitchen.

🔑 **Write like a Georgian** by using the quill and ink set.

Top Tip
There's a guide in every room who'll answer any questions you have. You could always ask if the staff still have to use bedpans when they need the loo!

← The Georgian House's kitchen

Fascinating Facts

★ The most junior female servants in Georgian houses were called scullery maids. They were as young as eleven years old and could work up to sixteen hours a day scrubbing floors.

★ The maid, who was supposed to be more senior, could still be as young as fourteen. Her job included emptying the bedpans – a sort of adult potty that people used in the days before toilets. *Poo*!

★ In those days there was no mains system and so people had their water delivered in barrels. This meant that things like baths were a luxury. Posh ladies wore a lot of perfume to hide the smell . . .

PLAN YOUR VISIT 39

The Georgian House
7 Charlotte Square, EH2 4ET
www.nts.org.uk/Property/56/

📞 0844 493 2118

🕐 Daily (summer) 10.00-18.00
(shorter hours out of season)

I want to go here ☐

WEST CENTRAL

EAST CENTRAL

NORTH

SOUTH & EAST

WEST

AROUND

TOP FIVES

SEEK OUT A SCULPTURE TRAIL

...at the Gallery of Modern Art

Here's a brief history of art . . . First came normal art, where artists tried to make their work look realistic. Then there was impressionism, when it became OK for art to look blurry and weird. Finally modern art arrived, and suddenly there were no rules at all.

The Gallery of Modern Art contains works by famous rule-breaking artists like Pablo Picasso and Tracey Emin. It also features the sculptures of Eduardo Paolozzi – a Scottish artist who was inspired by toys and games. So don't be a boring fart . . . seek out some modern art!

Sticker Scores

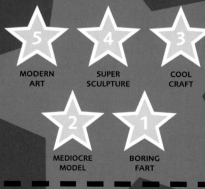

5 MODERN ART

4 SUPER SCULPTURE

3 COOL CRAFT

2 MEDIOCRE MODEL

1 BORING FART

Best Of The Rest

🔑 **Become part of the art** in the Dan Graham's *Two-Way Mirror*. It's a sculpture where you're the star!

Top Tip

If you enjoyed it, there are lots more art galleries in Edinburgh. The Scottish National Gallery of Modern Art, the National Gallery of Scotland and the Scottish National Portrait Gallery (re-opens 2011) are all nearby.

← Even the lawn is art

Why did the painter collapse?

Because he had an *art* attack!

Fascinating Facts

⭐ **One of Tracey Emin's most famous works of art (*My Bed*) basically just consists of her own unmade bed! So when you forget to make your own bed, tell your parents it's not laziness; it's art!**

⭐ A British artist called Chris Ofili uses *elephant poo* in his paintings. We told you there were no rules in modern art!

⭐ **The oldest known sculpture is over 35,000 years old. It's called the *Venus of Hohle Fels* and is an ivory carving of a woman.**

⭐ The most expensive sculpture ever sold is of the Greek goddess Artemis. It sold for nearly £15 million – that's enough to buy 15,000,000 tubs of Greek yoghurt!

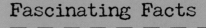

PLAN YOUR VISIT 40

Scottish National Gallery of Modern Art

75 Belford Road, EH4 3DR

www.nationalgalleries.org

📞 0131 624 6200

🕐 Daily 10.00-17.00

FREE ❌ 🎁 ☂

I want to go here ☐

WEST CENTRAL
EAST CENTRAL
NORTH
SOUTH & EAST
WEST
AROUND
TOP FIVES

HAVE AN ANCIENT EGYPTIAN ADVENTURE

...at Time Twisters

Ancient Egypt was not all fun and games. While the Egyptian pharaohs (rulers) lived in luxury, the workers who built the pyramids had to toil in back-breaking conditions.

Thankfully, despite the Egyptian theme, Time Twisters *is* all fun and games – because it's an awesome adventure play centre built on four levels! You can slide down a giant snake, swing across a swamp and crawl away from crocodiles.

Sticker Scores

5 — MARVELLOUS MUMMY

4 — FABULOUS PHARAOH

3 — SENSIBLE SCRIBE

2 — LAZY LABOURER

1 — CROCODILE TEARS

And all the time you're surrounded by Egyptian-style decorations.

There's also a sports area where you can play basketball and football . . . In fact, there are just *tomb* many options to list them all here!

WEST CENTRAL

EAST CENTRAL

NORTH

SOUTH & EAST

WEST

AROUND

TOP FIVES

Best Of The Rest

See if you're a super shot at the centre's shooting gallery. Fire foam balls at the targets using bright yellow guns.

Clamber up the climbing wall. See if you reach the top before you drop.

Take a ride on a bumpy slide. As well as the snake slides there's also an impressive two-floor wavy slide to hurtle down.

← Inside Time Twisters

Why was the Egyptian boy worried?
Because his daddy was a mummy.

Fascinating Facts

★ **Egyptian Pyramids are enormous buildings that are over 4,000 years old. Unsurprisingly they are shaped like a pyramid (you wouldn't have believed us if we'd said they were rectangular!) and were built to be burial tombs for the country's pharaohs.**

★ It took around 20 years and 100,000 people to build an Egyptian pyramid. That's enough people to fill Edinburgh's Murrayfield stadium 1.3 times! However, watching a Scotland rugby match is probably more fun than building an enormous, pointy burial tomb!

★ **It was so hot in Ancient Egypt that many children wouldn't bother wearing any clothes! However, we don't suggest you try this in Scotland – you're likely to either freeze to death or be arrested!**

PLAN YOUR VISIT 41

TimeTwisters

Unit 5 Catalyst Trade Park, 2b Bankhead Drive, EH11 4EJ

www.timetwisters.co.uk

📞 0131 308 2464

🕐 Daily 09.30-18.00

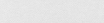

I want to go here ☐

KEY

● Places

▇ Parks

WEST CENTRAL

EAST CENTRAL

NORTH

SOUTH & EAST

WEST

AROUND

TOP FIVES

BRANDISH A BROADSWORD

...at Bannockburn

These days if the English and Scottish are engaged in battle, the setting is probably a football or rugby pitch. In 1314 things were different. In that year Scotland fought England at Bannockburn in a battle for independence from their pesky neighbours . . .

Bannockburn battlefield lies in Stirlingshire, west of Edinburgh. In the middle is an impressive statue of Robert the Bruce, the fearless king who led Scotland to a famous victory. Though Robert's army was greatly outnumbered, his men nevertheless gave the English a mighty thumping.

At the battlefield you'll also find a visitor centre where you'll get the chance to wield some weapons. Brandish a broadsword and then *ATTACK!* (Obviously don't actually attack anyone or you might get grounded!)

Sticker Scores

5	4	3
AXE WIELDER	SPEAR THROWER	ARROW AIMER

2	1
DAGGER DODGER	*AXE*-IDENT

WEST CENTRAL

EAST CENTRAL

NORTH

SOUTH & EAST

WEST

AROUND

TOP FIVES

← Statue of Robert the Bruce at Bannockburn

Best Of The Rest

🔑 Try on some chainmail. You can also dress up in medieval costumes if you don't want to fight like a knight.

🔑 Pick up a quiz from the visitor centre before you bound round the battlefield.

🔑 Enjoy the arts and crafts. The centre provides things to make and do on weekends and in school holidays.

Top Tip
You can only wield weapons when a history interpreter is present, so call ahead to check the schedule.

Fascinating Facts

⭐ A broadsword was a terrifying, two-handed blade that only the strongest soldiers could swing. They were designed for close combat, and were capable of slicing off an enemy's arm, leg, or head. You wouldn't want to use one to slice bread . . .

⭐ Chainmail was a form of armour made up from small metal rings linked together in a body suit. One set could weigh 30 kilograms which is the same as the average nine year old (but more likely to protect you in a battle)!

⭐ Bannockburn was perhaps the most important battle in a series of scraps for Scottish independence. However, some people think that the battle was elsewhere, as only one arrowhead has been found in the field.

PLAN YOUR VISIT 42

Bannockburn
Glasgow Road, Stirling, FK7 0LJ
www.nts.org.uk/Property/95/
📞 0844 493 2139
🕐 Daily 10.00-17.00
£ 🎁 ☂

I want to go here ☐

SAIL INTO THE SKY

...at the Falkirk Wheel

Sailing into the sky sounds impossible, but you can do it at the Falkirk Wheel. We reckon it will *float your boat*!

The Falkirk Wheel is an enormous, rotating structure that connects two canals at different heights. The wheel scoops up boats and lifts them between the canals, giving the vessels a giant helping hand.

You can take a ride in the wheel from the visitor centre. Board a boat and be amazed by the engineering as the wheel carries you from the Forth and Clyde canal up to the Union canal, 35 metres above. That's taller than a ten storey building!

Sticker Scores

5 COOL CANAL

4 LENGTHY LAKE

3 REGULAR RIVER

2 SMALL STREAM

1 ROOT CANAL

What sits on the bottom of the sea and shakes?

A nervous wreck.

Best Of The Rest

🔑 Scramble around the play area, which is just next to the wheel.

🔑 Take a trail to the Antonine Wall. This stretched from coast to coast in Scotland and was built by the Romans to keep out the Scots.

🔑 Hire a bike and cycle along the canal. Canals are particularly good for relaxed bike rides, because they're always so flat.

Top Tip
Book your boat trip online before you visit to guarantee getting tickets. Trips depart every 40-60 minutes.

← The Falkirk Wheel in action

Fascinating Facts

⭐ **The two pods that pick up the boats are known as gondolas. Their strange, water-slicing shape makes the wheel look a bit like a double-headed axe.**

⭐ The Falkirk Wheel's clever design means that each half-rotation uses just 1.5 kilowatts of energy. That's barely enough electricity to boil eight kettles. In other words, it's a *wheel*-y small amount!

⭐ **Each gondola holds 360,000 litres of water, or enough to fill a 25 metre swimming pool. However, we don't suggest you try doing a length in the gondola unless you want to be squished by a boat!**

PLAN YOUR VISIT 43

The Falkirk Wheel
Lime Road, Tamfourhill, Falkirk, FK1 4RS
www.thefalkirkwheel.co.uk
📞 08700 500 208
🕐 Most days 11.00-16.00
££ ❌ 🎁

I want to go here ☐

welcome to

WEST CENTRAL

EAST CENTRAL

NORTH

SOUTH & EAST

WEST

AROUND

TOP FIVES

SEE THE SHARKS

...at Deep Sea World

Getting up close to sharks is not normally something people recommend. However, at Deep Sea World you can safely stare a shark in the eye using their impressive underwater tunnel.

Deep Sea World is an aquarium full of fish and amphibious creatures. You'll see predatory piranhas, soppy seals and cool cichlids that are usually only found in Malawi, Africa.

Sticker Scores

5 SEAL SPOTTER

4 FISH FOLLOWER

3 CICHLID CHASER

2 BATFISH BOTHERER

1 SHARK SUPPER

Our favourite part is the underwater tunnel, where you can see the sharks being fed. Hold your nerve as the giant-toothed creatures swim towards you before devouring their lunch in one gulp. Just be glad there is 6.5cm of thick acrylic between them and you!

WEST CENTRAL

EAST CENTRAL

NORTH

SOUTH & EAST

WEST

AROUND

TOP FIVES

Best Of The Rest

Dive with sharks! If you're aged between eight and fifteen you can book a Bubblemaker session where you learn to scuba dive and then swim with real four metre sand tiger sharks in the aquarium's huge tank. The sharks are friendly, safe and they haven't eaten anyone. Yet . . .

← Sharks swimming overhead

Top Tip

The aquarium is a great place for birthday parties so bear it in mind if you're getting older in Edinburgh!

Fascinating Facts

★ Sharks were swimming in the sea 200 million years ago, when dinosaurs still roamed the earth. Unlike most animals, they've survived for millions of years without evolving much. One reason is that they're so good at finding and catching their next meal.

★ The smallest shark in the seas is the spined pygmy. It grows to around fifteen centimetres long. That's the same size as a small ruler (but less useful in a maths lesson!).

★ The largest shark in the world is the whale shark, which can be up to fifteen metres long. That's the length of one hundred pygmy sharks laid end to end! Fortunately, whale sharks don't eat people, so there's no need to *wail* if you get up close to one!

PLAN YOUR VISIT 44

Deep Sea World

Battery Quarry, North Queensferry, Fife, KY11 1JR

www.deepseaworld.com

📞 01383 411 880

🕐 Mon-Fri 10.00-17.00
Sat-Sun 10.00-18.00

£££ ✕ 🎁 ☂

I want to go here ☐

Who gives sharks pressies at Christmas?
Santa Jaws!

FIND FOOD FIT FOR A KING

...at Stirling Castle

Royal feasts take a good deal of preparation. You can't just stick some baked beans on a plate and serve them to a king. At Stirling Castle, you'll see how much effort was required to make a royal meal.

Stirling Castle was built in the 1500s by King James IV of Scotland. The building sits grandly on top of a volcanic hill (a bit like Arthur's Seat) and is a mightily impressive sight. And there's plenty to see once you're inside too.

We particularly like the Great Kitchens – you get a sense of how whole armies of servants would have prepared velvety venison and sumptuous salmon. You can even smell the scents that would have filled the King's kitchen. *Mmm!*

Sticker Scores

5 ROAST RABBIT

4 FRIED FISH

3 POACHED PARSNIPS

2 BAKED BREAD

1 BAKED BEANS

Best Of The Rest

🔑 Walk along the battlements and imagine yourself pouring boiling oil down on invaders.

🔑 See wartime weapons in the Regimental Museum, which is housed in the King's Old Building.

🔑 Watch the weavers in the Tapestry Studio. A team of experts are re-creating the castle's old tapestries – and you can watch them at work.

Why did the solider go mad?
Because he was regi-*mental*!

← The battlements at Stirling Castle

Fascinating Facts

⭐ **The first Scottish attempt at flying took place at Stirling Castle. In September 1507, John Damian jumped from the castle's walls with wings made of hens' feathers strapped to his back. Sadly he didn't fly, but he did break his thigh.**

⭐ The world's oldest surviving football was discovered in the rafters of the castle. It's from around 1540 and is made from leather and pig's bladder (that's the part of the pig where wee is stored).

⭐ **Within Stirling Castle there is a courtyard called the Lion's Den. Some people think it got the name because King James V kept a lion there . . . but we think they're *lyin'*! A more likely explanation is that lions often feature in Scottish coats of arms.**

PLAN YOUR VISIT 45

Stirling Castle
Castle Wynd, Stirling, FK8 1EJ
www.stirlingcastle.gov.uk

📞 01786 450 000

🕐 Daily (summer) 09.30-18.00
Daily (out of season) 09.30-17.00

££ ✗ 🎁

I want to go here ☐

WEST CENTRAL
EAST CENTRAL
NORTH
SOUTH & EAST
WEST
AROUND
TOP FIVES

FEED ANIMALS FROM A TRAIN

...at East Links Family Park

At some farms, trekking round to see all the animals can be a bit tiring. But East Links has come up with a clever solution – have a train line running through the animal enclosures!

East Links is stuffed full of things to do. As well as admiring the animals you can have fun in the huge fortress and run around the indoor play area.

However, our favourite part is the train safari.

LLAMA LUNCH

Sticker Scores

5 TERRIFIC TRAIN

4 EXCITING ENGINE

3 CHEERFUL CHOO CHOO

2 RUBBISH RAILWAY

1 SIGNAL FAILURE

Chug past sheep, look at llamas and peer at ponies while you ride around the circular railway route. Alternatively, burn off some energy by riding in one of the four-seater pedal cars. Either way, you can feed the animals as you travel. Grub's up!

Best Of The Rest

🔑 Struggle through the straw bales in the Hay Play Barn.

🔑 Take a pony ride. This is only available at peak times and costs extra – call ahead to check availability.

🔑 Hunt for hidden treasure on the pirate ship.

🔑 Test out the toboggan run, next to the goats in the centre of the park.

← Lunch, please!

Photo Op
Take a snap of you doting on a duckling in the animal handling area.

Fascinating Facts

★ One of the farm's most popular animals is Henry the Llama. Llamas spit when they are annoyed so we suggest you don't alarm a llama!

★ Within one hour of hatching, a duckling can see, walk, swim and feed. In comparison, within an hour of being born a baby human can . . . cry.

Top Tip
If you visit in the spring you can help feed the newborn baby lambs. Call in advance for details.

PLAN YOUR VISIT 46
East Links Family Park
Dunbar, East Lothian, EH42 1XF
www.eastlinks.co.uk

📞 01368 863607

🕐 Daily (summer) 10.00-18.00
Daily (out of season) 10.00-dusk

££

I want to go here ☐

WEST CENTRAL
EAST CENTRAL
NORTH
SOUTH & EAST
WEST
AROUND
TOP FIVES

CLIMB INSIDE A CONCORDE

...at the National Museum of Flight

Concorde was once the fastest way to get around. Sadly it doesn't fly anymore, so you can't take a trip on these super-speedy planes, but at the National Museum of Flight you can step inside one.

The National Museum of Flight is home to all kinds of aeroplanes, from wartime bombers through to jet airliners. It also has a real-life Concorde which used to fly between London and New York.

Sticker Scores

5 — CRACKING CONCORDE

4 — JUMBO JET

3 — AIRBUS

2 — GLIDER

1 — BIRD

Concorde was the first commercial plane capable of travelling at supersonic speeds. This means they could fly faster than the speed of sound, which is 761 miles per hour! You can step inside the museum's Concorde, check out its cockpit and wander under the wings. The hours will just *fly* by . . .

WEST CENTRAL

EAST CENTRAL

NORTH

SOUTH & EAST

WEST

AROUND

TOP FIVES

Best Of The Rest

🔑 Look for World War Two fighter planes. The museum owns a British Spitfire and a German Messerschmitt.

🔑 See the world's first passenger jet. The de Havilland Comet first flew in 1949 and could reach speeds of up to 490 miles per hour.

🔑 Find out how to fly an aeroplane in the Fantastic Flight area.

← What does this button do?

What do you call a flying policeman?
A heli-*copper*!

Fascinating Facts

★ **Concorde used 25,629 litres of fuel every hour. That's the same as 2,000 cars (but better at crossing the Atlantic)!**

★ In July 2000, a Concorde crashed shortly after take-off from Charles de Gaulle airport in Paris. 113 people were killed. The entire Concorde fleet was grounded while the cause of the crash was investigated. Though the planes did fly again for a while, Concorde flew for the last time on 24th October 2003 – a sad day for a supersonic plane.

★ **The longest golf shot ever was made down the aisle of Concorde in 1993. The ball went five miles in two seconds!**

PLAN YOUR VISIT 47

National Museum of Flight
East Fortune Airfield, East Lothian, EH39 5LF
www.nms.ac.uk

📞 0131 247 4238

🕐 Daily (summer) 10.00-17.00
Sat-Sun (out of season) 10.00-16.00

£ ✗ 🎁 ☂

I want to go here ☐

GO ON A SAFARI

...at Blair Drummond Safari Park

Blair Drummond is a dramatic drive-through experience. However, we're not talking about the sort of drive-through where you pick up lunch. We're talking about one where you can admire exotic animals.

There are lots of animals to see, and you can even stroke some of them (not the tigers, though). We particularly like safari parks because you get to see animals roaming around as if they were in the wild. At Blair Drummond you drive your car through the enclosures, just like on an African safari. Just make sure you don't get out, or you might find that you end up on the drive-through menu!

Sticker Scores

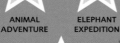

5 **SUPER SAFARI**

4 **ANIMAL ADVENTURE**

3 **ELEPHANT EXPEDITION**

2 **GIRAFFE JOURNEY**

1 **SNAIL TRAIL**

WEST CENTRAL

EAST CENTRAL

NORTH

SOUTH & EAST

WEST

AROUND

TOP FIVES

Best Of The Rest

🔑 **Look at lemurs** in the separate Lemur Land section. Stand beside the feeding tables or animal walkways to get a close-up view.

🔑 **Head to the Rhino House** and see Ailsa, the baby rhino who's growing up fast.

🔑 **Go wild in the Adventure Area.** You'll find pedal boats and an awesome aerial runway which lets you fly across a pond! You need to be 135 centimetres tall to use the aerial runway.

← Roaarrr!

What did the buffalo say when his kid left home?
Bye-son!

Fascinating Facts

★ **A lion's favourite food is zebra – they think you can't beat a bit of stripy meat. One zebra can feed a whole pride.**

★ In a herd of elephants, it is the women that are in charge. Presumably this means they make the male elephants do all the cleaning.

★ **Ostriches can run at up to 50 miles per hour for as long as half an hour. That's faster than your car is allowed to travel on most roads in Edinburgh!**

Photo Op
See if you can get a close-up snap of a lemur. They don't mind having an audience!

PLAN YOUR VISIT 48

Blair Drummond Safari and Adventure Park

Blair Drummond, Stirling, FK9 4UR

www.blairdrummond.com

📞 **01786 841 456**

🕐 **Daily 10.00-17.30**

££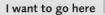

I want to go here ☐

WEST CENTRAL

EAST CENTRAL

NORTH

SOUTH & EAST

WEST

AROUND

TOP FIVES

TOP FIVE

...things to spot

If you look closely you'll find that Edinburgh is home to all kinds of unusual items and objects. So get your sightseeing specs on and see if you can spot the following local things.

I SPOTTED:

- ☐ Police boxes
- ☐ Pipers
- ☐ Kilts
- ☐ The old town wall
- ☐ Haggis

Police boxes

Don't worry, we're not suggesting that policemen belong in cardboard boxes! A police box is a blue telephone kiosk that was used by bobbies to report back to their local station.

One famous example is the Tardis in the TV show *Dr Who*. Nowadays the police boxes still dotted around Edinburgh function as things like coffee kiosks (on George Square) or even as a miniature art gallery (on St Leonard's Street).

Pipers

You won't have to look too hard to find a busker playing the bagpipes in Edinburgh – just open your ears!

Bagpipes are a loud, screechy instrument made out of a pipe attached to a big sack. Pipers can usually be found in the area around Princes Street and the Royal Mile. If you like them, chuck them some coins. If you don't, buy some earplugs!

WEST CENTRAL

EAST CENTRAL

NORTH

SOUTH & EAST

WEST

AROUND

TOP FIVES

Kilts

The old town wall

Haggis

In most places, you would be unlikely to see a man in a skirt . . . but in Edinburgh it happens all the time!

However, we don't mean a frilly cocktail frock. We're talking about the Scottish kilt – a pleated skirt with a tartan pattern. Kilts are usually worn on formal occasions, like ceilidhs (dances) and weddings. Pipers also wear them – so find a piper and you'll spot a kilt too!

For hundreds of years Edinburgh old town was surrounded by tall walls. This helped to prevent attacking armies and rampaging robbers from getting in.

Today you can still see the remains of the old walls. Look for the King's Wall down by Tweeddale Court (off the Royal Mile). Alternatively, you'll find the well preserved Flodden Wall on the corner of Drummond Street and the Pleasance, and running through Greyfriars Kirkyard.

In some countries, the national dish is an exquisite delicacy, made from the finest pieces of meat. In Scotland it's a blood-filled sausage made from sheep's stomach. *Mmm!*

Don't be put off by our description of a haggis though! It tastes a bit like a spicy sausage, and we'd definitely recommend trying some. The Standing Order on George Street serves Haggis for lunch and you can buy it in lots of shops around the city.

TOP FIVE

...festivals

One great thing about children's festivals in Edinburgh is that they're not all on at the same time. That means that whenever you come and visit there's a good chance that something special will be showing.

I WENT TO:

- [ ] Fringe Festival
- [ ] Science Festival
- [ ] Children's Book Festival
- [ ] Imaginate Festival
- [ ] Storytelling Festival

Fringe Festival

The Fringe is the world's largest arts festival, with thousands of shows competing for your attention. It happens during August as part of the hugely popular Edinburgh Festival.

The Fringe has a special kids' programme, which includes comedy, music, dancing and street performance. Order a catalogue from the website and pick out your favourite Fringe events. Don't forget to buy tickets in advance for popular shows as they can sell out quickly.

www.edfringe.com

Science Festival

If you're serious about science then Edinburg in April is the place to be. The Edinburgh International Science Festival is a two week science extravaganza packed with talks, tours workshops and general wackiness.

Past events have offered the opportunity to unwrap a mummy, build a body, play robot football or see a space show. You're also likely to be able to watch explosive experiments and all kinds of other fun (and frequently free) events.

www.sciencefestival.co.u

WEST CENTRAL

EAST CENTRAL

NORTH

SOUTH & EAST

WEST

AROUND

TOP FIVES

Children's Book Festival

Imaginate Festival

Storytelling Festival

The Children's Book Festival is part of the annual Book Festival that takes place in Edinburgh every August.

You can meet your favourite authors, check out new titles, and listen to one of the story sessions. There's also a special children's bookshop which has a reading area, and an activity corner for painting and drawing. Just don't scribble on the books or you might find yourself with a big bill!

If you're in Edinburgh in May then check out the children's theatre festival, called Imaginate.

Since 1988, groups from across the world have put on shows and workshops during this fun-filled, drama-driven week. Several venues and theatres take part – previous highlights include a puppet version of Cinderella and a comedy retelling of the story of Mary, Queen of Scots. We can't imagine-ate why anyone would miss it!

This festival is run by the Storytelling Centre (see p46) and is held at the end of October each year.

You can hear storytellers spinning yarns and telling tales during nine days of stories and song. We particularly like the Tell-a-Story day where children and adults get together to create and share stories. There are also Meet The Storyteller sessions and film screenings to keep you entertained.

www.edbookfest.co.uk

www.imaginate.org.uk

www.scottishstorytelling centre.co.uk

121

TOP FIVE

. . . toy and sweet shops

We put plenty of research into compiling this list of top toy and sweet shops. In fact, we seem to find ourselves going back to them again and again . . . just to check the standards are still high, of course!

Hawkin's Bazaar

Fudge Kitchen

If you've got money burning a hole in your pocket then we suggest you head to Hawkin's. Just make sure you put out the fire first or you'll end up with a burnt leg!

Hawkin's Bazaar is a top toy shop full of gadgets, gifts and games at pocket money prices. The shop has a 'do touch' policy, so you can try before you buy.

Hawkin's Bazaar

16 St James Shopping Centre, EH1 3SR
0844 573 4538
www.hawkin.com

At Fudge Kitchen you not only get the chance to try free fudge samples – you ca also watch it being mad right in front of you!

There are over twenty different fudge-tastic flavours including Double Trouble, Chocolate Orange and even Christmas Cake, s you're sure to find somethin you like. And if you don't have time to go there, you can always visit their websit and buy online.

Fudge Kitchen

30 High Street, Royal Mile, EH1
0131 5581517
www.fudgekitchen.co.uk

WEST CENTRAL

EAST CENTRAL

NORTH

SOUTH & EAST

WEST

AROUND

TOP FIVES

Wonderland Models

S. Luca

Helios Fountain

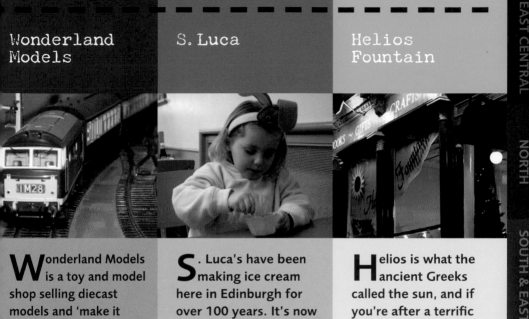

Wonderland Models is a toy and model shop selling diecast models and 'make it yourself' kits. It's the largest model shop in Scotland, so finding the right model is a doddle!

There are trains, tractors, touring cars, tanks, tornados . . . and even some things that don't begin with a 't'. They also stock things like doll's houses and board games – so you're unlikely to get *board* when you visit.

Wonderland Models
97/101 Lothian Road, EH3 9AN
0131 229 6428
www.wonderlandmodels.com

S. Luca's have been making ice cream here in Edinburgh for over 100 years. It's now eaten all over Scotland . . . and when you visit you'll quickly see why!

Both cafés stock loads of flavours of ice cream and sorbet alongside good Italian food. You'll also find their products in shops and restaurants all over the country.

S. Luca
16 Morningside Road, EH10 4DB
0131 446 0233
32-38 High Street, Musselburgh, EH21 7AG
0131 665 2237
www.s-luca.co.uk

Helios is what the ancient Greeks called the sun, and if you're after a terrific toy shop this place really shines.

Helios Fountain is on Grassmarket, near the castle, so it's a great place to stop off while you're doing some sightseeing. Alongside the wide range of toys you'll find charming crafts and brilliant beads. Our favourites are the wooden toys and puzzles – they'll brighten up your day!

Helios Fountain
7 Grassmarket, EH1 2HY
0131 229 7884
www.helios-fountain.co.uk

TOP FIVE

...places to run around

Edinburgh isn't short of green space, so you're always likely to be close to a perfect place to run around. All the parks we've listed welcome dogs too, so you'd be barking mad not to visit!

I WENT TO:

- [ ] The Meadows
- [ ] Saughton Park
- [ ] Colinton Dell
- [ ] Inverleith Park
- [ ] Leith Links

The Meadows

The Meadows used to be a swamp called the Burgh Loch. However, thankfully it was drained long ago so nowadays you won't sink when you visit!

There are three kids' playgrounds on the Meadows. They're all worth a visit, but our favourite is at the Hope Park Terrace end. You'll also find public tennis courts nearby, and a free pitch and putt golf course at the Bruntsfield Links end (summer only).

The Meadows
EH9

Saughton Park

Saughton Park on the west side of Edinburgh is another place with a great play park and loads of space to run around.

Once you've used up some energy, why not wander over to the Winter Garden, or step inside the tropical greenhouse where you can make a wish at the fish pond. Just don't blame us if it doesn't come true!

Saughton Park
Balgreen Road, EH11

WEST CENTRAL

EAST CENTRAL

NORTH

SOUTH & EAST

WEST

AROUND

TOP FIVES

Colinton Dell

Inverleith Park

Leith Links

Colinton Dell is part of the Water of Leith walkway. It's a pretty, wooded path alongside the river, and is a great spot for cycling, strolling or a spot of hide and seek.

Because the valley is wooded there are also all kinds of animals around. You can find a finch, watch a wren and observe an owl. Look out also for the disused train tunnel – it's *rail*-ly good fun to walk through!

Inverleith park is one of the biggest parks in Edinburgh. It's a great place to see swans and feed ducks. We think it's a *quacking* place to spend a day!

Check out the children's play area, or head over to the sundial garden to see a real sundial that's over 100 years old. Our favourite part is the pond – why not bring your own boat and sail it on the water?

Leith Links is a great park but in the past it has been a burial ground for plague victims and also a battlefield. The big mounds you can climb by Duncan Place were once gun positions!

Thankfully you're unlikely to see cannons being fired there today. However, you will find plenty of open space and a decent playground. Check out the giant climbing web at the Duncan Place end.

Colinton Dell
Off Lanark Road, EH14

Inverleith Park
East Fettes Avenue, EH4

Leith Links
Duncan Place, EH

TOP FIVE

...swimming pools

Edinburgh is set near some good beaches, so it is sometimes possible to swim in the sea. However, if you fancy some warmer water head to one of these great pools instead.

Leith Waterworld

Ride the waves and fly down the flumes at Leith Waterworld.

This leisure pool is built on the site of an old railway station and is the biggest pool in Edinburgh. The pool has various different areas to liven up your swim. Watch out for the water cannon, lie down in the lagoon or bathe in the bubble beds. *Water* great way to have fun!

Leith Waterworld

377 Easter Road, EH6 8HU
0131 555 6000
www.edinburghleisure.co.uk

Wester Hailes Education Centre

The Wester Hailes Education Centre is perfect for diving daredevils.

The pool is within a school, but it's open to the public every day. They've got a one metre and a two metre board, from which you can plunge into the pool below. At certain times of day during weekends and on holidays they also bring out an air slide and a giant inflatable island called the Gladiator Run. It's *splash*-tastic!

Wester Hailes Education Centre

5 Murrayburn Drive, EH14 2SU
0131 442 2201

WEST CENTRAL

EAST CENTRAL

NORTH

SOUTH & EAST

WEST

AROU.

Ainslie Park Leisure Centre

Portobello Swim Centre

Warrender Swim Centre

This is a nice friendly pool in the north of Edinburgh which is usually full of kids.

Have fun with the floats on Fridays and at weekends, or practise your paddling in their swim lanes. Once you've finished swimming you can warm up by jumping in the Jacuzzi or stewing in the sauna. Just don't stay sauna-ing for too long or you'll end up looking like a prune!

Ainslie Park Leisure Centre

92 Pilton Drive, EH5 2HF

0131 551 2400

www.edinburghleisure.co.uk

Alongside the normal swimming pools, Portobello swim centre also has a Turkish bath. Confusingly, you don't actually get wet, but you do get sweaty.

Turkish baths are steam baths. At Portobello Swim Centre there are three rooms at different temperatures from warm to really hot. Then, once you've worked up a sweat, there's also a cold pool to jump in. And, if you'd rather just do some swimming, there are two normal pools here too.

Portobello Swim Centre

57 The Promenade, EH15 2BS

0131 669 6888

www.edinburghleisure.co.uk

This is a lovely little pool with a big glass roof so when the sun's out it feels like you're swimming outside.

There are also Victorian changing cabins by the side of the pool – you almost expect to see people wearing old-fashioned, full body swimming costumes! The pool is just south of The Meadows (see p124) so you could combine your visit with some play in the park.

Warrender Swim Centre

Thirlestane Road, EH9 1AP

0131 447 0052

www.edinburghleisure.c

PARENTS' PAGE

- -

Greetings, adult. This page is all for you. The rest of the book's for kids, so we thought it was only fair that you had your own page. So if you're a child, stop reading. Now. We said stop. Look, the whole rest of the book's for you. This is just for adults. There's tons more interesting things to do in the rest of the book – why not go to p16 and find out how to tell the time using a gun? Honestly, that's got to be better than this page. So stop reading. OK, fine, alright then. Carry on. But don't say we didn't warn you.

So anyway, hello, adult.

Edinburgh Unlocked is for children who are visiting places with adults. Very few of our sites admit unaccompanied children. So as you're likely to be the one planning the trip, we've included site details, such as telephone numbers and opening hours, on each page. Bear in mind that most sites are closed for Christmas, and that last admission is usually earlier than the closing time. We've also specified if there are height or age restrictions. While we have tried hard to ensure all the details are accurate at the time of going to press, things change, so it's best to check before you go anywhere.

Next: the Internet. We've tried to make sure that all our websites are child-friendly, but all the same, we suggest you supervise any surfing. We take no responsibility for third-party content and we recommend you check a site first if you are at all unsure.

Now for some general tips:

- Quite a few venues run good workshops and activities during weekends and school holidays. These are sometimes free, but may require advance booking.

- Many of the activities can be combined into a single day out. Use the maps at the beginning of each section to work out what things are near each other.

- Some of the activities in our book could be dangerous without appropriate adult supervision. Children using this book should be accompanied at all times.

- Many of our free activities in Edinburgh involve walks or other locations which don't have opening hours. We recommend you only go during daylight, and make sure you leave enough time to complete the walks.

Oh, and we think it's worth us mentioning that none of the sites in this book pay to be included.

- -

Right then, that's the practical stuff out of the way, and there's still a page to fill. So we've selected some facts about Edinburgh just for grown-ups. We don't think they're as interesting as the facts in the rest of the book, but then being an adult you don't really like interesting facts do you now?

- Edinburgh was made a UNESCO World Heritage City in 1995. This means that a United Nations committee of adults decided that Edinburgh fulfilled the heritage and conservation criteria required for inscription on the World Heritage List. We're told adults are impressed by this sort of thing.

- There are various suggestions as to the etymology of the name Edinburgh. Some believe it is a derivation of the Anglo-Saxon for Edwin's Fort. Others think that it is a Celtic phrase meaning Fort of Eidyn. A final group of people do not care much either way.

- The original plan for Edinburgh New Town was for it to be shaped like a Union Jack, with the roads laid out to make a St George's and a St Andrew's cross.

- One of Edinburgh's most famous hills – the Mound – is actually man-made. Grown-ups built it in the 1700s using earth that was excavated from Nor Loch, where Princes Street Gardens can be found today. The Mound's name comes from the fact that it is an elephant. OK, OK. It's because it's a mound.

- Charles Dickens got his inspiration for the character of Scrooge in *A Christmas Carol* from an Edinburgh kirkyard (graveyard). He read the inscription on a grave as Ebenezer Lennox Scroggie Meanman when it actually said Mealman.

- 43.6% of the workforce in Edinburgh hold a degree or professional qualification; one of the highest percentages for a city in the UK.

- There are more FTSE 100 companies based in Edinburgh than anywhere else in the UK outside London. This makes it quite a good place for adults to get a job.

- Edinburgh is twinned with eleven world cities including Florence, Krakow, Munich and Vancouver.

- Edinburgh has a temperate maritime climate. It gets 1,350 hours of sunshine a year on average. It actually gets more sun than London during the winter months.

- Edinburgh is 56° north of the equator, which puts it on the same latitude as Moscow and Newfoundland. If you were to go to 56° south of the equator there would be no land at all on that latitude; just ocean.

- Edinburgh is an anagram of behind rug.

OK, that's your lot. Time to hand the book back to your child. Or, if you are a child who's read all of this, we hope you learned that reading stuff meant for adults just isn't going to be very funny.

INDEX

Here's an index of all the places included in

LLAMA LUNCH

the book, arranged in alphabetical order

WEST CENTRAL

EAST CENTRAL

NORTH

SOUTH & EAST

WEST

AROUND

TOP . . .

INDEX

Where can you . . .

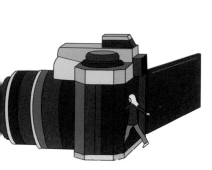

...see cool stuff?

...make the most of a short stay?

WEST CENTRAL

EAST CENTRAL

NORTH

SOUTH & EAST

WEST

AROUND

TOP FIVES

BACK-OF-THE-BOOK QUIZ

Good Luck!

The answers to all the following questions can be found somewhere in Edinburgh Unlocked. Email a correct set of answers to us and you'll have a chance to win a signed and framed illustration of your choice from the book!

1 What (and where) is the Stone of Scone?

2 Why is Dolly the sheep famous?

3 What's the difference between a mercat and a meerkat?

4 Where in Edinburgh is there a time ball, and at what time of day does it drop?

5 How long is Europe's longest aerial runway?

6 Why did sailors on the HMY *Britannia* use hand signals?

A. Because the engines were so noisy that they couldn't always hear each other
B. Because they wanted their own secret language that no other sailors could understand
C. Because they didn't want to disturb resting royals

7 What did golf balls used to be made of?

A. Feathers
B. Grass
C. Clay

8 What do butterflies use to taste things?

A. Their antennae
B. Their feet
C. Their wingtips

9 The Olympic sport of curling involves

A. Skidding stones across ice
B. Throwing a ball round a corner
C. Making straight hair curly

10 Which places are on the same latitude as Edinburgh?

A. Moscow and Newfoundland
B. Helsinki and Greenland
C. Notsureland and Dontknowia

Tie-breaker

In no more than 30 words, tell us what is your favourite place in the book and why.

Send your answers to **quiz@factfinderguides.co.uk**

Full terms and conditions are on our website.

Colin Chisholm

Colin wasn't very keen on working when he was at school, so naturally he became a teacher. He loves stories and writing, provided he can choose what he writes about and the deadlines are flexible. He's very pleased that he has been able to write about kids' stuff in Edinburgh as he's been working with children there for nearly eight years. His favourite Edinburgh excursion is walking along the Hermitage of Braid, preferably with the family dog.

Emily Kerr and Joshua Perry

Colin refers to Josh and Emily as Jemily. They quite like this, as they have known each other since school and often finish each other's sentences. Jemily are big fans of Edinburgh and the surrounding area. Emily has been to the festival lots of times and thinks the Falkirk wheel is awesome. Josh frequently visits the city to see his sister and once conducted a meeting next to the flying fox in Dalkeith Country Estate.

Katherine Hardy (Kardy)

Kardy used to want to operate fairground rides for a living, but she has since settled for being an illustrator instead. She loves Edinburgh, and sang jazz and blues at the Fringe one year. When she was a child, she had a mackerel thrown at her by one of the festival performers. Quentin Blake has described her drawings as "strong and subtly nuanced". This is also not a bad description of her personality.

Allison Curtis

Allison was once part of a successful world record to have the most people bouncing on space hoppers at the same time. She likes dogs (a lot). Allison went to Edinburgh once when she was a child and remembers playing in the snow. She likes the idea of walking through the waves to get to Cramond Island, and might try it on a space hopper some time.

CREDITS

Author: Colin Chisholm
Series Editors: Emily Kerr, Joshua Perry
Design: Allison Curtis

Illustrations: Katherine Hardy
Maps: Allison Curtis, with reference to
OpenStreetMap – a free, editable map of the world

Thank you to ...

Colin

Emma Hall for thinking of me when she first heard about *Edinburgh Unlocked* from Emily. The children at St Cuthbert's RC Primary and in the 75th Blackford cub scout pack for being my eager market-research guinea pigs. All the kids who've ever been part of the Tuesday night Children's Holiday Venture group for making sure that not only do I know the best places for kids in Edinburgh but also know what it is that makes them great. Various colleagues at St Cuthbert's and Forthview Primary Schools for telling me about places their classes or their own children had loved. Friends with kids/grandkids who sent me a steady stream of "is x in?" emails. Steven Hider for helping me to find the fun (and aiding alliteration). My flatmates Paul and David Atherton for accompanying me on some of the research trips and being available to look sympathetically at early drafts. Finally to my parents whose personal help I could take for granted but whose professional experience was an immense bonus too. Thank you Dad for keeping my drafts grounded with a sense of history and perspective ("you can't put that in!") and thank you Mum for your exhaustive editorial comments and stylistic queries ("I've got no idea what you're trying to say here").

Emily, Josh, Kardy and Allison

Everyone who helped us with the first two books. Rory Neeson, Harry Petrushkin, and Katie Brewis for being a series of seriously fantastic flatmates. And Rory for his thoughts on the spine. Nadine and Tony for helping with some last-minute proofing. Little Curtis for loving the jokes (and suggesting some new ones), and of course Big Curtis, always. Those cute little red squirrels for their determined survival. Will Taylor for great advice and ongoing support. Anna Somers Cocks for suggestions and enthusiasm. Cornelia O'Donovan, Siobhan Hewlett, Bella Hird, and Radio 4 for work-time entertainment. Ian, Carla, and our mums and dads for their continued confidence and fiscal friendliness. The Sufi monks of Yemen for discovering coffee and sharing their knowledge with the world. The flickr photographers for their photos. Hannah Perry for putting up with our continued bafflement in the face of her explanations as to what a company secretary actually does.

Photo Credits

11 flickr, Morgan Johnston	65 flickr, Stuart Caie	119 flickr, J E Theriot
13 Camera Obscura and World of Illusions	67 flickr, Jon Connell	119 flickr, Tyler Krob
15 Mary King's Close	71 flickr, Paweł B k	119 flickr, zoonabar
17 flickr, Jordan S Hatcher	73 Dalkeith Country Park	120 flickr, Cassio Cricor
19 The Edinburgh Dungeon	75 flickr, Andrew Girdwood	120 flickr, Horia Varlan
21 National Museums Scotland	77 Dark Ocean	121 flickr, Paull Young
23 Museum on the Mound / Paul Zanre	79 flickr, Geoff Wong	121 flickr, Steve Snodgrass
25 Edinburgh Bus Tours	81 flickr, Wojciech Kulicki	121 flickr, Nina Hale
27 Mercat Tours	83 Dobbies Garden Centres	122 Hawkin's Bazaar,
29 Edinburgh Winter Wonderland	85 Scottish Mining Museum	122 flickr, Andrew Barden
31 Edinburgh Military Tattoo	89 flickr, Kabsik Park	123 flickr, Dave_S
35 flickr, William Marnoch	91 flickr, Cristian Bortes	123 S. Luca
37 flickr, Gnomonic	93 National Trust for Scotland Photo Library	123 flickr, Megan Talarmo
39 flickr, William Marnoch	95 Rzss	124 flickr, Jack_g
41 City of Edinburgh	97 flickr, J Lord	124 flickr, Clear Spot
43 City of Edinburgh	99 Time Twisters	125 flickr, OliBac
45 Our Dynamic Earth	103 National Trust for Scotland Photo Library	125 flickr, Kodok
47 Scottish Storytelling Centre	105 British Waterways Scotland	125 flickr, Victoria Cormie
49 City of Edinburgh	107 Deep Sea World	126 flickr, Steve Jurvetson
51 flickr, Lyn Gateley	109 flickr, mdid	126 flickr, Casey Yancey
53 flickr, Martin Pettitt	111 flickr, Ian Wilson	127 flickr, Lee Coursey
55 Scottish Parliamentary Corporate Body	113 National Museums Scotland	127 flickr, The Consumerist
59 flickr, Stuart Caie	115 Blair Drummond Safari Park	127 flickr, Ashleigh290
61 Alien Rock	118 flickr, Zenilorac	
63 The Royal Yacht Britannia	118 flickr, Sheep Purple	